STRATEGIES for Writers

Level E

Authors

Leslie W. Crawford, Ed.D.
Georgia College & State University

Rebecca Bowers Sipe, Ed.D.
Eastern Michigan University

ZB
Zaner-Bloser

Educational Consultants

Barbara Marinak
Reading Supervisor
Mechanicsburg, PA

Catherine C. Thome, Ed.D.
English/Language Arts and Assessment Coordinator
Educational Services Division
Lake County Regional Office of Education
Grayslake, IL

Science Content Reviewer

Michael Grote, Ed.D.
Math and Science Education
Columbus Public Schools
Columbus, OH

Teacher Reviewers

Janice Andrus, Chanhassen, MN
Shannon Basner, Hollis, NY
Teressa D. Bell, Nashville, TN
Victoria B. Casady, Ferguson, MO
Kristin Cashman, Mechanicsburg, PA
Jeanie Denaro, Brooklyn, NY
Susan H. Friedman, Ph.D., Sharon, PA
Katherine Harrington, Mechanicsburg, PA
Dianna L. Hinderer, Ypsilanti, MI

Eleanor Kane, Stow, OH
Jean Kochevar, Minneapolis, MN
Diane L. Nicholson, Pittsburgh, PA
Susan Peery, San Antonio, TX
David Philpot, San Francisco, CA
Jodi Ramos, San Antonio, TX
Jacqueline Sullivan, Sunnyvale, CA
Rita Warden-Short, Brentwood, TN
Roberta M. Wykoff, Stow, OH

Page Design Concepts and Cover Design

Tommaso Design Group

Photo Credits

Models: George C. Anderson Photography

p12, Craig Tuttle, Corbis Stock Market; p19, Kunio Owaki, Corbis Stock Market; p20, Peter Griffith, Masterfile; p43, Craig Tuttle, Corbis Stock Market; p46, Digital Vision, PictureQuest; pp49, 50, George C. Anderson Photography; p59, Arthur S. Aubry, PhotoDisc, PictureQuest; p61, Stephen McBrady, PhotoEdit, PictureQuest; p67, Photo 24, Brand X Pictures, PictureQuest; p70, Doug Handel, Corbis Stock Market; p85, S. Solum, PhotoLink, PhotoDisc, PictureQuest; p89, Carol Christensen, Stock South, PictureQuest; pp89, 96, Jeff Foott, Discovery Images, PictureQuest; p107, Photo Sphere Images, PictureQuest; p119, Victor Aleman, Black Star Publishing, PictureQuest; pp129, 193, Corbis Images, PictureQuest; p137, John Coletti, Stock, Boston, Inc., PictureQuest; p149, Andre Jenny, Focus Group, PictureQuest; p171, Andre Jenny, Focus Group, PictureQuest; p201, Craig Tuttle, Corbis Stock Market; p213, Courtesy NASA; p233, Stephen Webster, Worldwide Hideout, Inc.

Art Credits

pp21, 23, 25, Bill Ogdon; pp35, 36, 37, Jack Kershner; pp86, 87, 88, 159, 160, 161, Dave Blanchette; pp163, 165, Ruth Flanagan; pp197, 217, Lori Champney; p214, Rita Enos-Castaldini; HB7, HB8, HB9, HB11, HB24, HB25, HB42, Marilyn Rodgers Bahney Paselsky; HB12, Brooke Albrecht; HB16, Pat DeWitt Grush.

Production, Photo Research, and Art Buying by Laurel Tech Integrated Publishing Services

ISBN 0-7367-1235-6

Zaner-Bloser, Inc., P.O. Box 16764, Columbus, Ohio 43216-6764 (1-800-421-3018)

Printed in the United States of America   03   04   05   06   104   5   4   3   2

NARRATIVE
writing

Personal Narrative

Writing Model:
"Don't Call Me Goldilocks". II

Rubric I4

Prewriting

Gather: Look at photographs to
get ideas. Pick a photo that reminds me
of a personal experience.. 20
Organize: Organize my thoughts
in a storyboard. 21

Drafting

Write: Draft the body of my personal
narrative by writing one or more
sentences about each picture on
my storyboard. 22

Revising

Elaborate: Write an introduction
and a conclusion that will interest
my reader. 24
Clarify: Replace overused words and
clichés with more exact words and
fresh language.. 26

Editing

Proofread: Make sure I have avoided
run-on sentences by joining compound
sentences correctly. 28

Publishing

Share: Submit my personal narrative
to a magazine. 30

Eyewitness Account

Writing Model:
"The New Madrid Earthquake". 35

Rubric 38

Prewriting

Gather: Draw on my memory of an
incident. Jot down what I saw
and heard.. 44
Organize: Make a sequence chain
of the most important events. 45

Drafting

Write: Draft my account by writing
one paragraph for every part of
my sequence chain. 46

Revising

Elaborate: Add quotes to make
my account more interesting. 48
Clarify: Make sure the order of
sentences in each paragraph
is logical. 49

Editing

Proofread: Check for the correct
forms of all pronouns. 50

Publishing

Share: Present my eyewitness account
in a classroom "TV news broadcast." . 52

3

DESCRIPTIVE

writing

Descriptive Essay

Writing Model:
"Sarah, the Sound Engineer" **59**
Rubric **62**

Prewriting

Gather: Think about people who interest me. Gather information about their personalities, appearance, and interests. **68**
Organize: Use my notes to make a spider map. **69**

Drafting

Write: Draft my description. Begin by describing the most interesting thing about my topic. **70**

Revising

Elaborate: Add similes to make my description clearer. **72**
Clarify: Combine short, choppy sentences. **73**

Editing

Proofread: Check to see that plural nouns and possessive nouns are formed correctly. **74**

Publishing

Share: Publish my descriptive essay in a class newsletter. **76**

Observation Report

Writing Model:
"New Mexico Piñon Pines" **79**
Rubric **80**

Prewriting

Gather: Take notes on what I am observing. **86**
Organize: Organize my notes into a network tree. **87**

Drafting

Write: Draft my report. For each main point in my network tree, write a topic sentence and add details. **88**

Revising

Elaborate: Fill in any gaps in my description. **90**
Clarify: Make sure my sentences begin in a variety of ways. **91**

Editing

Proofread: Check to see that all subjects and verbs agree. **92**

Publishing

Share: Record my report in an observation journal. **94**

EXPOSITORY
writing

Research Report

Writing Model: "Chief Joseph" 101
Rubric 102

Prewriting

Gather: Take notes from the Internet and at least one other source. Cite my sources. 108
Organize: Use my notes to make a support pattern. 110

Drafting

Write: Draft the body of my report. Write a paragraph for each main point on my organizer. 112

Revising

Elaborate: Complete my report by adding an introduction and a conclusion. 114
Clarify: Delete any unnecessary information. 115

Editing

Proofread: Check to see that I have capitalized words correctly. 116

Publishing

Share: Include my written report in my multimedia presentation to the class. . . 118

Compare-and-Contrast Essay

Writing Model: "Television Goes to the Movies" 123
Rubric 124

Prewriting

Gather: Interview others and take notes. 130
Organize: Organize my interview notes into an attribute chart. Include my own ideas, too. 131

Drafting

Write: Draft my essay. Discuss the likenesses and differences in separate paragraphs. 132

Revising

Elaborate: Make sure the information I add helps to develop an unbiased presentation. 134
Clarify: Rewrite stringy sentences to make them clearer. 135

Editing

Proofread: Check to see that all titles are capitalized and punctuated correctly. 136

Publishing

Share: Put my essay in a time capsule. 138

NARRATIVE

writing

Fable

Writing Model:
"The Fox and the Crow" 143

Rubric 144

Prewriting

Gather: Pick a fable that interests me.
Take notes on it so I can rewrite it
in my own words. 150
Organize: Organize the plot events
using a cause-and-effect chain. 151

Drafting

Write: Draft my retelling of the fable.
Make sure the causes and effects
are clear. 152

Revising

Elaborate: Add dialogue to make the
story and characters come alive. . . . 154
Clarify: Make sure all the plot events
lead to the moral of the fable. 155

Editing

Proofread: Check to see that I
have not used double negatives. 156

Publishing

Share: Illustrate my fable and make
it into a book for the classroom
library. 158

Mystery

Writing Model:
"The Case of the Disappearing Soccer
Shirt" 163

Rubric 166

Prewriting

Gather: Brainstorm some people
and events for my mystery. 172
Organize: Make a story map to
plan my mystery. 173

Drafting

Write: Draft my mystery, using the story
map and paying special attention
to the clues. 174

Revising

Elaborate: Add suspenseful words.
Use a thesaurus to find new words. . . 176
Clarify: Check for conflicting
information. 177

Editing

Proofread: Check to see that I have
punctuated quotations correctly. 178

Publishing

Share: Read my mystery to the class
on Authors' Day. 180

PERSUASIVE

writing

Book Review

Writing Model:
And Now Miguel by Joseph Krumgold . **187**

Rubric **188**

Prewriting

Gather: As I read my book, take notes on ideas I might include in my review. **194**

Organize: Use my notes to make a pros-and-cons chart. **195**

Drafting

Write: Draft my book review, starting with my thesis statement. **196**

Revising

Elaborate: Include quotations and examples to support my opinion. **198**

Clarify: Restate my opinion at the end of the book review. **199**

Editing

Proofread: Make sure pronoun antecedents are clear. Check to see that pronouns agree with their antecedents in number. **200**

Publishing

Share: Submit my book review to a literary magazine. **202**

Letter to the Editor

Writing Model:
Letter About Recycling **207**

Rubric **208**

Prewriting

Gather: Use what I read and learn from others to form an opinion about a topic. **214**

Organize: Make an outline to focus and support my opinion. **215**

Drafting

Write: Draft my letter to the editor. State my opinion, support it, and sum up my argument. **216**

Revising

Elaborate: Add reasons and facts to support my opinion. **218**

Clarify: Add signal words to clarify my ideas. **219**

Editing

Proofread: Check that I have written all six parts of a business letter correctly and that there are no sentence fragments. **220**

Publishing

Share: Submit my essay to a newspaper or magazine. **222**

writing

Analyze the Writing Prompt

Writing Model: "Tell Me a Story" **229**

Prewriting

Gather: Read and analyze the writing prompt. Make sure I understand what I am supposed to do. **234**

Organize: Plan my time. **236**

Gather and Organize: Choose a graphic organizer. Use it to jot notes. **237**

Organize: Check my graphic organizer against the Scoring Guide. **238**

Drafting

Write: Use my network tree to write an explanation with a good introduction, body, and conclusion. **240**

Revising

Elaborate: Check what I have written against the Scoring Guide. Add any missing facts or details. **242**

Clarify: Check what I have written against the Scoring Guide. Make sure I have used signal words so that everything is clear. **243**

Editing

Proofread: Check that I have used correct grammar, capitalization, punctuation, and spelling. **244**

test tips **247**

Extra Practice

Conventions & Skills

CS 1

Writer's HandBook

HB 1

NARRATIVE

writing

tells the reader a story.

1
Personal Narrative

2
Eyewitness Account

NARRATIVE writing

Personal Narrative

In this chapter, you will practice one kind of narrative writing: the **personal narrative**.

In a **personal narrative,** the writer tells a true story about his or her own life.

The story on the next page is a personal narrative. Study the following questions. Then read the personal narrative, keeping the questions in mind.

 **Does the writer capture and keep the reader's interest?**

 **How well is the story organized?**

 **Do the introduction and the conclusion add to the narrative?**

 **Does the writer choose words that are exact and fresh instead of overused words and clichés?**

 **Are all compound sentences joined correctly?**

DON'T CALL ME GOLDILOCKS

by Jackie Haley

Do you have a nickname? I do, and it's an absolutely horrible one. Everybody calls me Goldilocks! It wouldn't be so bad if I had blond, curly hair and fair skin. However, my hair is black, and my skin is dark. So how did I get this nickname? It all started on a family vacation at Yellowstone National Park.

Yellowstone is spectacular. It has towering waterfalls, dramatic canyons, crystal-clear lakes, bubbling pools of boiling water and colorful mud, and incredible geysers that shoot steam and hot water high into the air. The wildlife is definitely not tame, and animals wander freely throughout the park. You can see lumbering bison, stately elk, soaring eagles, cutthroat trout, and graceful trumpeter swans. Naturally, Yellowstone also has bears.

On our first day at Yellowstone, my parents decided to plan all of our daily excursions. While they studied hiking and geological maps, I went outside for a walk. They told me to stay near the lodge; they also warned me about the bears. However, I wandered off, following a stream into a wooded area. It was cool, quiet, and dark underneath the trees. I was really enjoying my walk until I heard a loud snap!

I jerked my head in the direction of the noise, but I didn't see a thing. Then the leaves rustled, and I saw something move. When I finally saw what it was, I froze on the spot. Three grizzly bears were looking right at me. The first bear was huge and looked ferocious. The second bear was not quite as large, and the third was a baby bear that would have looked cuddly—in a zoo!

I couldn't move a muscle, but my mind was racing. What did my parents say about bears? How was I supposed to get away from them? I tried to calm down. The bears didn't look too unhappy; that was good. I remembered that Mom said bears have a good sense of smell and bad eyesight. I hoped I didn't smell too good, and I really hoped they couldn't see me very well. She had also said that bears could run over 30 miles per hour. I took a deep breath and decided that I was in serious trouble.

I don't know how long I stood there, but it seemed like forever. I was starting to panic when I heard a low voice say, "Stay calm. I'm right behind you." I cannot tell you how happy I was to hear Dad's voice! He said not to look at the bears; he told me to back away quietly and carefully. As I moved backward very slowly, I knew the three bears were watching me closely.

After several long minutes, Dad said, "I think we're okay now, so turn around and follow me. Don't say a word until I do." When we reached the clearing, he grabbed me and hugged me. "What were you thinking?" he asked in a voice that shook a little. "You could have been killed!"

What could I say? I glanced back and breathed a long sigh of relief. The bears weren't anywhere in sight.

As we hurried toward the lodge, Dad turned to me and said, "Guess we'll have to call you Goldilocks from now on. You could have gotten into a lot of trouble with those three bears today." I sighed; I knew what was coming. Dad went in and announced to everyone that he had saved me. He described the three bears and my predicament in great detail and with elaborate gestures. I got lots of hugs and lectures that afternoon, and, unfortunately, I also got a nickname.

Using a Rubric

Have you ever used a rubric? A rubric is a good way to assess a piece of writing. Rubrics are easy to use. You simply assign 1, 2, 3, or 4 points in each category in the rubric.

Remember the questions that you studied on page 10? Those questions were used to make the rubric you see here.

66 Hi! My name is Janell. I'm learning how to write a personal narrative, too. What did you think about the story on pages 11–13? Let's use this rubric to figure out how well the story was written. Review the questions in each category in the rubric. Next, read the scoring information for each category. Then, on pages 16–18, we will use this rubric to assess the story. 99

Does the writer capture and keep the reader's interest?

How well is the story organized?

Do the introduction and the conclusion add to the narrative?

Does the writer choose words that are exact and fresh instead of overused words and clichés?

Are all compound sentences joined correctly?

Narrative Writing • Personal Narrative

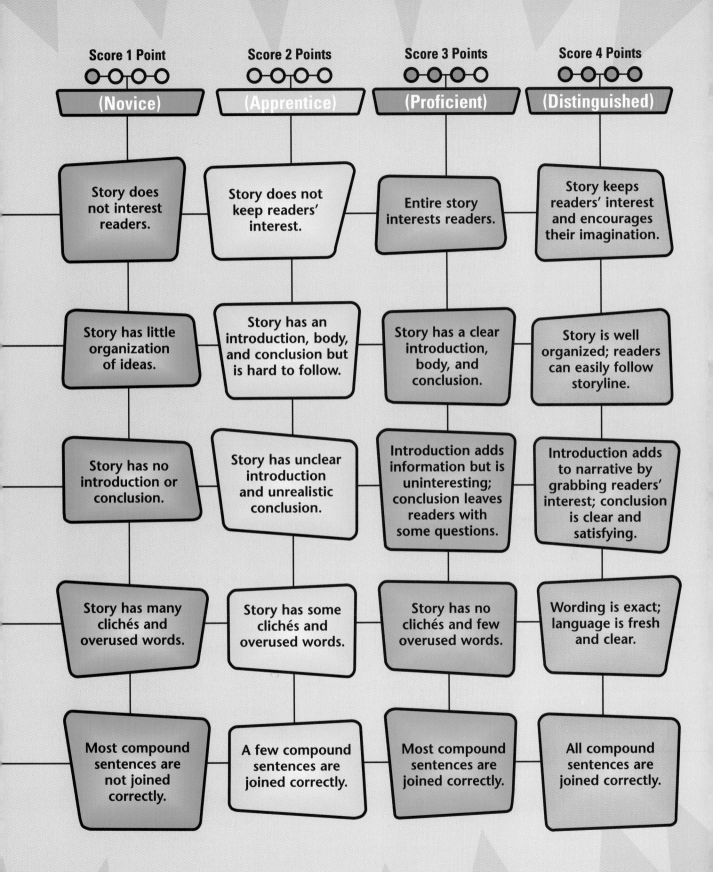

Score 1 Point	Score 2 Points	Score 3 Points	Score 4 Points
(Novice)	**(Apprentice)**	**(Proficient)**	**(Distinguished)**
Story does not interest readers.	Story does not keep readers' interest.	Entire story interests readers.	Story keeps readers' interest and encourages their imagination.
Story has little organization of ideas.	Story has an introduction, body, and conclusion but is hard to follow.	Story has a clear introduction, body, and conclusion.	Story is well organized; readers can easily follow storyline.
Story has no introduction or conclusion.	Story has unclear introduction and unrealistic conclusion.	Introduction adds information but is uninteresting; conclusion leaves readers with some questions.	Introduction adds to narrative by grabbing readers' interest; conclusion is clear and satisfying.
Story has many clichés and overused words.	Story has some clichés and overused words.	Story has no clichés and few overused words.	Wording is exact; language is fresh and clear.
Most compound sentences are not joined correctly.	A few compound sentences are joined correctly.	Most compound sentences are joined correctly.	All compound sentences are joined correctly.

Using a Rubric
to Study the Model

Use the rubric to assess Jackie's story. Remember, you will give 1, 2, 3, or 4 points in each category.

How many points did you give Jackie's story in each category? Discuss each category on the rubric with your classmates. Find words and sentences in the story that support each answer you gave. Then read Janell's assessment of the story.

Audience

Does the writer capture and keep the reader's interest?

> In the introduction, the writer makes you curious about her nickname. She makes you believe that she has an interesting story to tell about why she's called Goldilocks.

Do you have a nickname? I do, and it's an absolutely horrible one. Everybody calls me Goldilocks! It wouldn't be so bad if I had blond, curly hair and fair skin. However, my hair is black, and my skin is dark. So how did I get this nickname? It all started on a family vacation at Yellowstone National Park.

Organization

How well is the story organized?

> The writer tells the story in chronological order. In other words, she tells the story's events in the order in which they happened. The story has a clear introduction, body, and conclusion.

On our first day at Yellowstone, my parents decided to plan all of our daily excursions. While they studied hiking and geological maps, I went outside for a walk. They told me to stay near the lodge; they also warned me about the bears. However, I wandered off, following a stream into a wooded area. It was cool, quiet, and dark underneath the trees. I was really enjoying my walk until I heard a loud snap!

Elaboration

Do the introduction and the conclusion add to the narrative?

> When I explained the Audience category of the rubric on page 16, I mentioned how the writer used her introduction to get the reader interested in the story. The writer also wrote a conclusion that makes sense and provides a good ending for the story.

As we hurried toward the lodge, Dad turned to me and said, "Guess we'll have to call you Goldilocks from now on. You could have gotten into a lot of trouble with those three bears today." I sighed; I knew what was coming. Dad went in and announced to everyone that he had saved me. He described the three bears and my predicament in great detail and with elaborate gestures. I got lots of hugs and lectures that afternoon, and, unfortunately, I also got a nickname.

Clarification — Does the writer choose words that are exact and fresh instead of overused words and clichés?

> The writer did not include clichés or overused words. Instead, she used exact and vivid words. They made the story sound fresh and clear.

Yellowstone is spectacular. It has towering waterfalls, dramatic canyons, crystal-clear lakes, bubbling pools of boiling water and colorful mud, and incredible geysers that shoot steam and hot water high into the air.

Conventions & Skills — Are all compound sentences joined correctly?

> Yes, the writer has formed compound sentences by using both commas with conjunctions and semicolons.

I couldn't move a muscle, but my mind was racing. What did my parents say about bears? How was I supposed to get away from them? I tried to calm down. The bears didn't look too unhappy; that was good.

❝ Now it's my turn to write!

> I'm going to write my own personal narrative. Follow along, and you will see how I use good writing strategies. I will also use the model story and the rubric to guide my writing.

JaNeLL

Writer of a
Personal Narrative

Name: Janell

Home: southern West Virginia

Hobbies: swimming, white-water rafting, writing in my journal

Favorite Book: *Strange Mysteries From Around the World* by Seymour Simon

Assignment: personal narrative

Prewriting

Gather

Look at photographs to get ideas. Pick a photo that reminds me of a personal experience.

❝ I'm a rafter! That's what you call people who use rafts to travel on rivers. I live near the New River Gorge National River in West Virginia. My family goes white-water rafting whenever we can. Over the years, my parents have taught me all about staying safe on rivers. Rafting can be dangerous, so I need to know what I'm doing.

"When my teacher asked us to write personal narratives, I decided to look at pictures of rafting in our family album. I knew that those pictures would help me remember some of my experiences. I discovered that I had many good stories locked up in my memory! ❞

Go to page 6 in the **Practice** the Strategy **Notebook!**

Prewriting

Organize

Organize my thoughts in a storyboard.

> I know from the **Rubric** that organization is important. When I looked at the pictures, I remembered so many stories. There was so much to tell! I decided to make a storyboard. A storyboard could help me organize my thoughts. Then I could write a great story about rafting!

Storyboard

A **storyboard** is a series of pictures. The pictures show the main events of a story in the order they happen.

Go to page 8 in the **Practice the Strategy Notebook!**

Drafting

Write

Draft the body of my personal narrative by writing one or more sentences about each picture on my storyboard.

"Now I'm ready to write! I remember from the **Rubric** that it is important to get organized. It also reminded me that I need to think about my audience. My family and my classmates will be my audience.

"I want my readers to raft on the river with me! I need to include good descriptions in the body of my story. The readers should feel the cold water and hear the waves. They should be excited and scared just like I was. As I draft my story, I'll do my best to avoid mistakes in spelling or grammar. However, I won't worry if I make some errors. I will check for mistakes later."

Body

The **body** is the main part of a story. The body comes between the introduction and the conclusion. It develops the main ideas and events in a story.

1

Mom, Dad, and I wore swimsuits, T-shirts, old sneakers, windbreakers, and sunglasses. We also had on safety helmets and life jackets.

2

We rented a yellow raft. Dad and Mom paddled our raft down the river, and I enjoyed the ride.

3

When we got to a place where the water was calm and still, Dad decided to fish.

4

Dad's hook got caught on rocks or something under the water, and our raft capsized in the river. We all fell in. So did the paddles, fishing rod, and the fish.

Go to page 9 in the **Practice** the Strategy **Notebook!**

Revising

Elaborate

Write an introduction and a conclusion that will interest my reader.

> After I wrote my first draft, I remembered from the **Rubric** that a good introduction makes a story better.
>
> "That's true! I will hook my friends with a great beginning. They will love to read my story about rafting!

Introduction

The **introduction** is the beginning of a story. A good introduction grabs the reader's attention. It makes the reader eager for the story to unfold.

[2nd DRAFT]

"We're going to have a relaxing day." That's what Dad said as we left our house. I was nine years old, and this was my first raft trip. Our plan was to raft down the calmer part of the New River. Mom and I were planning to enjoy the ~~ride~~ scenery and get some sun; Dad was going to fish. He had promised that we would go rafting on rougher rapids some day, but I needed to get some experience on calmer water first. Then he said those words ~~another~~ a second time: "We're going to have a relaxing day." Was he ever wrong!

READ TO A PARTNER

"Then I wanted another opinion, so I read my draft to my friend Alisha. She said it was really interesting, but it needed a conclusion. How could I have forgotten? The **Rubric** said that a narrative must have a clear and satisfying conclusion. Here's what I wrote."

Conclusion

The **conclusion** is the end of a story. It ties up loose ends and summarizes the action.

When we got home that night, we were ~~really~~ completely exhausted. Our clothes were still damp, and our bruises were beginning to ~~hurt~~ ache. Naturally, we didn't have ~~one~~ a single fish. We were all smiling, though. Every time one of us mentioned our "relaxing" day and all the fish Dad had caught, we started laughing again. Mom called Dad's promise of a relaxing day "famous last words." Perhaps he should have said, "This will be a day we'll never forget!"

Go to page 10 in the **Practice the Strategy Notebook!**

Revising

Clarify

Replace overused words and clichés with more exact words and fresh language.

" When I read my story, it didn't seem interesting, and the words sounded ordinary. I decided to make some revisions, or changes. I removed clichés and other words that I had used too often. I replaced them with more interesting and exact words. "

Cliché

A **cliché** is a phrase that has been used over and over. Here are some examples:

- as smart as a fox
- few and far between
- as pretty as a picture
- a tower of strength

Overused Words

Overused words include *said, beautiful, nice,* or *good.* Overused words should be replaced with words that have more meaning. For example, *said* could be replaced with *explained, shouted, whispered,* or *mumbled.*

When we got to the New River, Dad rented a yellow raft and two

paddles. Mom and Dad's task was to steer the raft with the pad-

dles; my task was simply to ~~sit there like a bump on a log and~~ enjoy

delete cliché

a swimsuit, T-shirt, shorts, old sneakers, a windbreaker,

the ride. Each of us wore ~~rafting clothes,~~ sunglasses, and sunscreen.

We also put on helmets to protect our heads and life jackets to

keep us afloat, just in case. We were well prepared and ready to

delete cliché

go! ~~I was as happy as a lark!~~

more exact words

got off to a good start   paddled down the river

more interesting words   We ~~started down the river.~~ We ~~moved~~ through some small waves

that were ~~as~~ easy to handle ~~as taking candy from a baby.~~ Next, we

encountered   (sp) channel

~~ran into~~ a narrow ~~chanel~~ where the water moved more swiftly. Finally,

perfectly still   **replace cliché**

more exact word   we came to a place where the river was ~~as smooth as glass.~~ We

peacefully   quite a while, and we began to feel the warm

floated ~~there~~ for ~~a long time. The sun was bright, and my skin got~~

rays of the sun beating down upon us. Eventually

~~hot. Then,~~ Dad handed me the paddle and said, "You hold this for a

more interesting words

while. I'm going to fish."

Go to page 12 in the **Practice** the Strategy **Notebook!**

Editing

Proofread

Make sure I have avoided run-on sentences by joining compound sentences correctly.

> Now I am going to check my story for errors. I think my story is good, but proofreading will make it even better. I need to correct spelling, punctuation, and capitalization, and I will check to see that I have avoided run-on sentences. I need to make sure that all compound sentences are joined correctly. I don't want any of these errors to confuse my readers.

Forming Compound Sentences

Short, related sentences may be joined with a comma followed by a coordinating conjunction (*and, but,* and *or*) or with a semicolon. The two sentences become one **compound sentence**.

Examples of Compound Sentences:

Dad threw his line in the water, **and** he quickly caught a fish.

Dad threw his line in the water; he quickly caught a fish.

A compound sentence that is joined incorrectly is called a **run-on**.

Examples of Run-ons:

Dad threw his line in the water, he quickly caught a fish.

Dad threw his line in the water he quickly caught a fish.

Extra Practice
See **Forming Compound Sentences**
(pages CS 2–CS 3) in the back of this book.

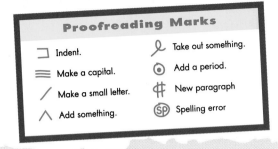

Proofreading Marks

⌐ Indent.

≡ Make a capital.

／ Make a small letter.

∧ Add something.

ℒ Take out something.

⊙ Add a period.

New paragraph

SP Spelling error

[4th DRAFT]

creating a
compound sentence

SP threw

Dad ~~through~~ his line into the water ~~by the side of the raft,~~ and he

immediately caught a fish. It was a small-mouth bass. He cast his line

again, and soon he had a Muskie. Then he landed another and

another and another. The fish were everywhere! Then it happened∧

,but

Dad's hook got caught on something big. It was probably a rock∧we

thought it might be a huge fish. "watch out!" he yelled, "I'm going

to need some room!" ~~When Dad yells, he is really loud.~~ #Just then, we

into some waves

noticed that our boat was drifting. The water wasn't so calm any-

more. Mom started to say something∧but Dad completely lost his bal-

,

ance. He toppled over∧and the raft rocked ~~really~~ wildly back and

,

forth! His fishing rod flew up in the air, and the raft started to cap-

size. Water rushed over the sides of the raft, and we quickly began

SP bail

to ~~bale~~ it out with our hands. suddenly the raft flipped over! We

tumbled into the ~~really~~ cold water; we banged into rocks, the raft,

and each other.

creating a
compound sentence

the Strategy

Go to page 13 in the **Practice**∧**Notebook!**

Publishing

Share
Submit my personal narrative to a magazine.

Writer: Janell

Assignment: personal narrative

Topic: white-water rafting

Audience: students who like to read true stories

Method of Publication: submit to magazine

Reason for Choice: to share my adventure with other students

" I like to read other students' writing in magazines, so I decided to submit my story to **Highlights for Children**. I think their readers would enjoy my story. Here's what I did to submit my story. "

1. I made a very neat, double-spaced copy of the final draft of my story.

2. I wrote a business letter to *Highlights for Children* telling them that I would like to submit my story for publication in their magazine.

3. Then I got an envelope and wrote the following address on it:

   Highlights for Children
   803 Church Street
   Honesdale, PA   18431

   I also included a stamped, self-addressed envelope.

4. I put a stamp on the envelope and mailed my letter and my story to *Highlights for Children*.

Famous Last Words

by Janell

"We're going to have a relaxing day." That's what Dad said as we walked out our door on a spectacularly sunny morning. I was nine years old, and this was my first raft trip. Our plan was to raft down the calmer part of the New River. Mom and I were planning to enjoy the scenery and get some sun; Dad was going to fish. Dad promised that we would go rafting through rougher rapids some day, but he said that I needed to get some raft experience on calmer water first. Then he said those words a second time: "We're going to have a relaxing day." Was he ever wrong!

When we got to the New River, Dad rented a yellow raft and two paddles. Mom and Dad's task was to steer the raft with the paddles; my task was simply to enjoy the ride. Each of us wore a swimsuit, T-shirt, shorts, old sneakers, a windbreaker, sunglasses, and sunscreen. We also put on helmets to protect our heads and life jackets to keep us afloat, just in case. We were well prepared and ready to go!

We got off to a good start. We paddled down the river through small waves that were easy to handle. Next, we encountered a narrow channel where the water moved more swiftly. Finally, we came to a place where the river was perfectly still. We floated peacefully for quite a while, and we felt the warm rays of the sun beating down upon us. Eventually, Dad handed me the paddle and said, "You hold this while I fish."

Dad threw his line into the water, and he immediately caught a fish, a small-mouth bass. He cast his line again, and soon he had a muskie. Then he landed another and another and another. The fish were everywhere! Then it happened; Dad's hook got caught on something big. It was probably a rock, but we thought it might be a huge fish. "Watch out!" he yelled. "I'm going to need some room to get my line loose!"

Just then, we noticed that our boat was drifting into some waves that weren't so calm. Mom started to say something, but Dad completely lost his balance. He toppled over, and the raft rocked wildly back and forth! His fishing rod flew up in the air, and the raft started to capsize. Water rushed over the sides of the raft, and we quickly began to bail it out with our hands. Suddenly the raft flipped over! We tumbled into the cold water, banging into rocks, the raft, and each other. Then we noticed that everything was floating away. We managed to snag the paddles and the fishing rod, but the lucky fish were long gone. We struggled to turn the raft right side up and finally crawled in. We were soaking wet and more than a little cranky!

By the time we got home that night, we were completely exhausted. Our clothes were still damp, our bruises were beginning to ache, and we didn't have a single fish. We were all smiling, though. Every time one of us mentioned our "relaxing" day and all the fish Dad caught, we started laughing again. Mom called Dad's promise of a relaxing day his "famous last words." Perhaps he should have said, "This will be a day we'll never forget!"

Janell Smith
123 Main St.
Pleasantview, WV 12345

Highlights for Children
803 Church Street
Honesdale, PA 18431

USING the Rubric for Assessment

Go to pages 14–15 in the **Practice the Strategy Notebook!** Use that rubric to assess Janell's paper. Try using the rubric to assess your own writing.

NARRATIVE
writing

Eyewitness Account

In this chapter, you will practice another kind of narrative writing: the **eyewitness account**.

In an **eyewitness account,** the writer gives a true and accurate report of an event that he or she directly observed.

The story on the next page is an eyewitness account. Study the following questions. Then read the eyewitness account, keeping the questions in mind as you read.

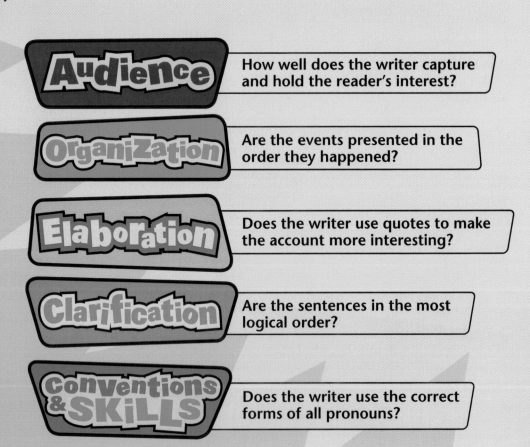

Audience — How well does the writer capture and hold the reader's interest?

Organization — Are the events presented in the order they happened?

Elaboration — Does the writer use quotes to make the account more interesting?

Clarification — Are the sentences in the most logical order?

Conventions & Skills — Does the writer use the correct forms of all pronouns?

The New Madrid Earthquake

by Henry Lang

My name is Henry Lang, and I used to own a small farm near New Madrid, Missouri. Most people from New Madrid will tell you that the most memorable day of their lives was December 16, 1811. That was the day the first earthquake hit. Looking back, I can see the warnings and signs, but no one heeded them then, and many lives were destroyed that day.

The year 1811 was unusual. A comet appeared in March, and astronomers said that this particular one hadn't been seen for 3,065 years. As the comet's streak grew brighter and brighter, some people became frightened. Some even predicted that the world was coming to an end.

We had a solar eclipse in June that year, too. As the sun slowly disappeared, the day became as dark as night.

Then there was the strange behavior of the animals. Huge flocks of pigeons and parrots ate the crops in our fields. The day before the earthquake, all the animals on my farm acted strangely. Other farmers say they saw squirrels drown themselves in the rivers as they tried to leave the area.

"Something's wrong here," I said. "What on earth is happening?" Well, something was wrong, but it wasn't on the earth. It was deep within the earth.

I was sleeping soundly on the night of December 15 when the house began to shake, moving my bed violently back and forth. I was tossed on the floor, with my leg bent under me. I heard my leg break, and a sharp pain hit me. All this time, the ceiling was collapsing, and the walls were cracking and falling. A sound like thunder welled up from beneath the house, deep within the earth. Then I heard my neighbors shrieking and calling, "Help us! Save us!" I wanted to get up and help them, but the pain in my leg was too fierce.

I don't know exactly how long the earth quaked that night. It seemed like hours to me. The air was moist and smelly, and even my candle couldn't shine through the thick darkness. I lay on the floor alone, waiting and wondering.

Smaller tremors hit throughout the night, but by morning the air had cleared. When I managed to crawl outside, I couldn't believe my eyes. Trees were split, homes were destroyed, fires burned, and injured people wandered around in disbelief. The ground had opened up near my house, and the gaping crack was filled with a thick, brown bubbling substance. My neighbors and I agreed on one thing that day. Never before had we seen a sight so fearsome or so grim.

That night was the beginning of many tremors along the Mississippi River valley. A large earthquake struck again in January. In February, we had the worst one. It caused the strangest things to happen. It temporarily turned a part of the Mississippi River into a waterfall, and another section of the river ran backwards for a while. That's when I decided to leave New Madrid for good.

Today I live in Ohio. Putting my life back together hasn't been easy, but eventually I saved enough money to buy more farmland. The day I paid for it, I looked at my new fields and said, "No one ever owns the land. It has a life and mind of its own. We only get to use it for a while."

Using a Rubric

Have you ever used a rubric? A rubric is a good way to assess an author's writing. Rubrics are easy to use. You simply assign 1, 2, 3, or 4 points in each category that the rubric identifies.

Remember the questions that you studied on page 34? Those questions were used to make the rubric you see here.

"Hi! My name is William. I'm learning how to write an eyewitness account, too. What did you think about the eyewitness account on pages 35–37? Let's use this rubric to figure out how well the eyewitness account of the New Madrid earthquake was written.

"Study the rubric. Review the questions in each category. Next, read the scoring information for each category. Then, on pages 40–42, we'll use this rubric to evaluate the eyewitness account."

Audience

How well does the writer capture and hold the reader's interest?

Organization

Are the events presented in the order they happened?

Elaboration

Does the writer use quotes to make the account more interesting?

Clarification

Are the sentences in the most logical order?

Conventions & Skills

Does the writer use the correct forms of all pronouns?

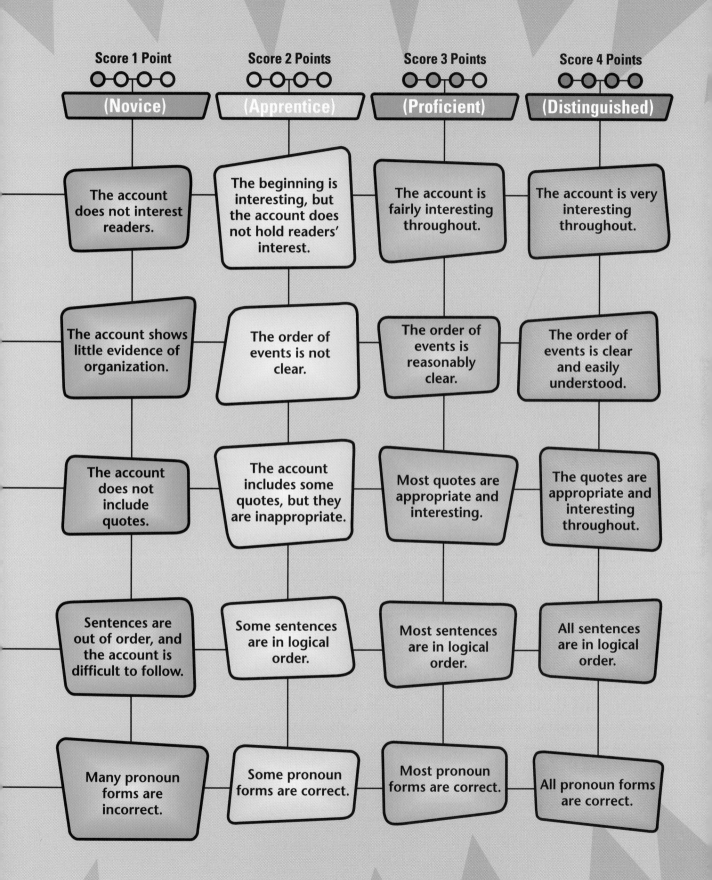

Score 1 Point
(Novice)

Score 2 Points
(Apprentice)

Score 3 Points
(Proficient)

Score 4 Points
(Distinguished)

The account does not interest readers.

The beginning is interesting, but the account does not hold readers' interest.

The account is fairly interesting throughout.

The account is very interesting throughout.

The account shows little evidence of organization.

The order of events is not clear.

The order of events is reasonably clear.

The order of events is clear and easily understood.

The account does not include quotes.

The account includes some quotes, but they are inappropriate.

Most quotes are appropriate and interesting.

The quotes are appropriate and interesting throughout.

Sentences are out of order, and the account is difficult to follow.

Some sentences are in logical order.

Most sentences are in logical order.

All sentences are in logical order.

Many pronoun forms are incorrect.

Some pronoun forms are correct.

Most pronoun forms are correct.

All pronoun forms are correct.

Using a Rubric to Study the Model

Use the rubric to assess the eyewitness account of the New Madrid earthquake. Remember, you will give 1, 2, 3, or 4 points in each category.

How many points did you give the eyewitness account? Discuss each category on the rubric with your classmates. Find words and sentences in the account that support your evaluation in each category. Then read William's assessment of the eyewitness account.

Audience

How well does the writer capture and hold the reader's interest?

66 The writer wrote an introduction that made me curious. I wondered what the warnings and signs were and what happened when the earthquake struck. As I kept reading, I wondered what would happen next. 99

My name is Henry Lang, and I used to own a small farm near New Madrid, Missouri. Most people from New Madrid will tell you that the most memorable day of their lives was December 16, 1811. That was the day the first earthquake hit. Looking back, I can see the warnings and signs, but no one heeded them then, and many lives were destroyed that day.

Organization

Are the events presented in the order they happened?

> This eyewitness account is written in chronological order. For example, after telling about the earthquake in December, the writer tells about the one in January and the one in February.

That night was the beginning of many tremors along the Mississippi River valley. A large earthquake struck again in January. In February, we had the worst one. It caused the strangest things to happen. It temporarily turned a part of the Mississippi River into a waterfall, and another section of the river ran backwards for a while. That's when I decided to leave New Madrid for good.

Elaboration

Does the writer use quotes to make the account more interesting?

> The writer uses several quotes to make the people in the account come alive. At the end of the story, I was interested in the quotation from himself that he included. It made him sound sadder but wiser.

Today I live in Ohio. Putting my life back together hasn't been easy, but eventually I saved enough money to buy more farmland. The day I paid for it, I looked at my new fields and said, "No one ever owns the land. It has a life and mind of its own. We only get to use it for a while."

Clarification

Are the sentences in the most logical order?

> This writer definitely put his sentences in logical order. In the paragraph below, the first sentence says that the writer's bed moved around violently. This leads to the second sentence, which says these violent movements tossed the writer on the floor. If these sentences were in a different order, I would sure be confused!

I was sleeping soundly on the night of December 15 when the house began to shake, moving my bed violently back and forth. I was tossed on the floor, with my leg bent under me. I heard my leg break, and a sharp pain hit me. All this time, the ceiling was collapsing, and the walls were cracking and falling.

Conventions & Skills

Does the writer use the correct forms of all pronouns?

> Yes, the writer used the correct pronouns. For example, I noticed that he named himself last by writing 'My neighbors and I agreed....' That's a hard rule for me to remember. I have to be careful not to write 'I and my neighbors agreed...' or even 'My neighbors and me agreed....'

My neighbors and I agreed on one thing that day. Never before had we seen a sight so fearsome or so grim.

Now it's my turn to write!

> I'm going to write my own eyewitness account. Follow along as I use good writing strategies. I will also use the model eyewitness account and the rubric to guide me.

WILLIAM

Writer of an Eyewitness Account

Name: William
Home: southern Illinois
Hobbies: fishing, reading
Favorite Sport: soccer
Favorite Book: *Hatchet* by Gary Paulsen
Assignment: eyewitness account

Prewriting

Gather

Draw on my memory of an incident. Jot down what I saw and heard.

> I grew up hearing stories about floods. My hometown was located in a floodplain of the Mississippi River, and it had been flooded in 1910, 1943, 1944, and 1947. People always said that there would be another flood, but no one was prepared for the next flood! I wasn't very old when the Mississippi River flooded my hometown, but, boy, do I remember it well!
>
> "When my teacher asked us to write an eyewitness account, I chose to write about the flood. I decided to gather my thoughts by writing down what I saw and heard during the flood. I included all the important details I could remember."

What I Saw and Heard During the Flood

- the river moving closer and closer
- kids playing in the rain every day
- the rain hitting our roof night and day
- people trying to save the town with sandbags
- the entire town covered by water
- almost everything destroyed
- a huge lake where the town used to be
- long lines of cars leaving town
- my town getting rebuilt

Go to page 16 in the **Practice** the Strategy **Notebook!**

Prewriting

Organize Make a sequence chain of the most important events.

" I know from the **Rubric** that organization is important. I remembered a lot of things about the flood, but my memories weren't organized. I decided to make this sequence chain to help organize my thoughts. Then I could write an accurate eyewitness account of the flood. "

Sequence Chain

A **sequence chain** shows steps or events in the order they happen.

The Flood

First Event:	hearing that a flood was coming our way
Next Event:	getting ready to leave our house in case of a flood
Next Event:	getting evacuated at the end of July
Next Event:	finding out how much damage the flood had caused
Next Event:	beginning a cleanup, but getting more flooding in September
Final Event:	watching the town get rebuilt in a higher, safer place

Go to page 18 in the **Practice the Strategy Notebook!**

Drafting

Write

Draft my account by writing one paragraph for every part of my sequence chain.

"Now I'm ready to write! I want my readers to see and hear and feel what the flood was like. I will write a paragraph for every event in my sequence chain so my readers can easily follow what happened. You can read the first part of my draft on the next page. As I draft my account, I won't worry about making mistakes in spelling or grammar. I'll write now and check for mistakes later."

Paragraph

A **paragraph** is a group of sentences that focus on one main idea or thought.

The Flood

First Event: hearing that a flood was coming our way

That summer, I heard stories on the news about broken levees and floods upstream. I knew that the Mississippi had flooded many times in the past. I heard that Valmeyer had been flooded in 1910, 1943, 1944, and 1947. I wondered if this was the year that it would happen again.

Next Event: getting ready to leave our house in case of a flood

The rain fell steadily that year. During June and July, my friends and I played in the rain almost every day. My mother worried as the water rose. I got boxes from the grocery store. I walked around those boxes for weeks. She would look around our house and frown. Then she began to make lists. She said that we had to decide what we'd take if we had to leave. She said that we needed to decide now. She and I filled the boxes with important papers, photographs, and other favorite things.

Next Event: getting evacuated at the end of July

At the end of July, we were evacuated. The flood was on its way. My father and me loaded the boxes into the car. Then we packed some clothes and left. As we drove away, we stared sadly at our house.

Go to page 20 in the **Practice** the Strategy **Notebook!**

Revising

Elaborate

Add quotes to make my account more interesting.

> Quotes make an eyewitness account more interesting. I learned that from the **Rubric**, too. I thought about all the things I had heard people say during the flood. I decided to use some of those quotes in my account. Here's how I did it.

Quotation

A **quotation** (often called a **quote**) is a speaker's exact words.

Example: "When is this rain going to stop?" she asked.

Use quotation marks at the beginning and end of the quotation. Place the end punctuation before the last quotation mark. Use a comma to set off the quotation from the rest of the sentence.

[2nd DRAFT]

quotation

Valmeyer, my hometown, is a small town located in the floodplain

of the Mississippi River. I grew up hearing all about floods. In fact,

"One day," they said, "the great Mississippi River is going to
my grandparents predicted the flood that changed Valmeyer forever.
come calling. No one beats the powerful old Mississippi!"

Stories of broken levees and floods upstream filled the news dur-

ing that summer. I knew that the Mississippi had flooded many times

in the past. Valmeyer itself had been flooded in 1910, 1943, 1944,

I heard people say, "This is the year!" I wondered if they were right.
and 1947. quotation

Go to page 22 in the **Practice** the Strategy **Notebook!**

Revising

Clarify

Make sure the order of sentences in each paragraph is logical.

" When I read my account, something didn't sound right. I read it again and realized that some of my sentences were out of order. This made my description confusing. After I put the sentences in a more logical order, my account was much easier to follow! "

reordered sentences

[3rd DRAFT]

My mother worried as the water rose. I got boxes from the grocery store. I walked around those boxes for weeks. She would look around our house and frown. Then she began to make lists. "We have to decide what we'll take if we have to leave. We can't take everything, so let's decide now." She and I filled them with important papers, photographs, and other favorite things.

Go to page 23 in the **Practice** the Strategy **Notebook!**

Editing

Proofread
Check for the correct forms of all pronouns.

> I know from the **Rubric** that I should pay attention to conventions and skills. Now it's time! I always check my spelling, capitalization, and punctuation when I proofread. Today I'll pay special attention to the correct forms of pronouns. I'll also look to see if I put the words **I** and **me** last when I wrote about another person and myself. You can see some of my changes on page 51.

Forms of Pronouns

The **subject pronouns** are *I*, *he*, *she*, *we*, and *they*.

    I saw the water rising. **They** ran for higher ground.

The **object pronouns** are *me*, *him*, *her*, *us*, and *them*.

    The water raced toward **us,** and a large wave hit **him**.

    The words **you** and **it** can be used as subject and object pronouns.

Possessive pronouns such as *my*, *his*, *her*, *your*, *our*, *its*, and *their* show ownership.

    My umbrella would not open, so **our** clothes got soaked.

When you write about yourself and another person, always name the other person first.

    Incorrect: I and **Steve** sat together.

    Correct: Steve and **I** sat together.

Extra Practice
See **Forms of Pronouns** (CS 4–CS 5) in the back of this book.

Proofreading Marks

⌐ Indent.

≡ Make a capital.

/ Make a small letter.

∧ Add something.

ℓ Take out something.

⊙ Add a period.

⌗ New paragraph

(SP) Spelling error

[4th DRAFT]

When the floodwaters came, Valmeyer disappeared. It was gone, gone, gone. Muddy brown water, twenty feet deep in some places, covered everything. Homes were destroyed, (SP) roads were washed out, and farms were underwater. My friends and I saw so many things floating in the water—furniture, toys, telephone poles, trees, and parts of houses. When the vice president of the United States visited the flooded areas, he was shocked to see how much of the land was underwater. "It's as if another Great Lake has been added to the Map of the United States!" he said.

correct pronoun form

The floodwaters receded, and the cleanup began. Then in september, it happened again. This time, flooding completely destroyed Valmeyer. I remembered my grandparents' prediction. "no one beats the powerful old Mississippi! they had said. I was beginning to think they were right. They had been right about the snowstorm last winter, too. However, The story of Valmeyer has a happier ending than you might expect. Valmeyer did beat the (SP) Mississippi River. It relocated! The citizens of Valmeyer met with federal officials and decided to move the entire town. The government helped us rebuild Valmeyer high above the floodplain. It now sits on a bluff that overlooks its old location. So (SP) there are really two Valmeyers, the old and the new. The other residents of Valmeyer and I don't need to worry about floods anymore.

correct pronoun form

correct pronoun form

Go to page 24 in the **Practice** the Strategy **Notebook!**

Publishing

Share

Present my eyewitness account in a classroom "TV news broadcast."

> **Writer:** William
> **Assignment:** eyewitness account
> **Topic:** the flooding of Valmeyer, Illinois
> **Audience:** classmates
> **Method of Publication:** oral presentation
> **Reason for Choice:** to share my eyewitness account as if I were on a television news program

> " I like to watch the news on television. I especially like it when a reporter gives an eyewitness account. Here's what I did to turn my eyewitness account into a TV news broadcast. "

1. I used my computer to make a neat copy of my account. I made it easy to read by putting extra space between lines.

2. I wrote this introduction to my news story: "Hello! My name is William, and I am here with an update on the flooding in Valmeyer, Illinois."

3. I practiced reading the introduction and the account aloud. I even recorded myself on a tape recorder. I made sure to speak clearly and not rush.

4. I put a table and chair at the front of the classroom.

5. I made a cardboard sign with the name of a TV station. Then I put the sign on the table facing the audience.

6. I presented the eyewitness account as if I were really on television.

Higher and Drier
by William

I'm standing on a bluff overlooking the Mississippi River. I am in the town of Valmeyer, Illinois. I am also looking down upon the town of Valmeyer, Illinois. How is that possible? Let me tell you about the flood that hit when I was little.

Before the flood, Valmeyer, my hometown, was located in the floodplain of the Mississippi River. I grew up hearing all about floods. In fact, my grandparents predicted the flood that changed Valmeyer forever. "One day," they said, "the great Mississippi River is going to come calling. No one beats the powerful old Mississippi!"

Stories of broken levees and floods upstream filled the news during that summer. I knew that the Mississippi had flooded many times in the past. Valmeyer itself had been flooded in 1910, 1943, 1944, and 1947. I heard people say, "This is the year!" I wondered if they were right.

The rain fell steadily on the Mississippi Valley that year. It rained for 49 days straight. I wasn't very old, but I remember those rains. During June and July, my friends and I played in the rain almost every day. Sometimes we'd help the people fill sandbags to protect our town in case it flooded. The river was usually four miles from town. However, it was creeping closer every day.

My mother worried as the water rose. She would look around our house and frown. Then she began to make lists. "We have to decide what we'll take if we have to leave. We can't take everything, so let's decide now." I got boxes from the grocery store. She and I filled them with important papers, photographs, and other favorite things. I walked around those boxes for weeks.

At the end of July, we had to leave. The flood was on its way. My father and I loaded the boxes and some clothes into the car. As we drove away, we stared back at our house. "We'll be safer on higher ground," my father said sadly.

When the floodwaters came, Valmeyer disappeared. Muddy brown water, twenty feet deep in some places, covered everything. Homes were destroyed, roads were washed out, and entire farms were underwater. My friends and I saw so many things floating in the water—furniture, toys, telephone poles, trees, and parts of houses. When the vice president of the United States visited the

Narrative Writing • Eyewitness Account

flooded areas, he was shocked to see how much of the land was underwater. "It's as if another Great Lake has been added to the map of the United States!" he said.

The floodwaters receded, and the cleanup began. Then in September, it happened again. This time, flooding completely destroyed Valmeyer. I remembered my grandparents' prediction. "No one beats the powerful old Mississippi!" they had said. I was beginning to think they were right.

However, the story of Valmeyer has a happier ending than you might expect. Valmeyer did beat the Mississippi River. It relocated! The citizens of Valmeyer met with federal officials and decided to move the entire town. The government helped us rebuild Valmeyer high above the floodplain. It now sits on a bluff that overlooks its old location. So there are really two Valmeyers, the old and the new. The other residents of Valmeyer and I don't need to worry about floods anymore.

USING the Rubric for Assessment

Go to page 26 in the **Practice ∧ Notebook!** Use that rubric to assess
                              the Strategy
William's paper. Try using the rubric to assess your own writing.

your own NARRATIVE writing

Science

Put the strategies you practiced in this unit to work to write your own personal narrative, eyewitness account, or both! You can:

- develop the writing you did in the Your Own Writing pages of the *Practice the Strategy Notebook*;
- pick an idea below and write something new;
- choose another idea of your own.

Be sure to follow the steps in the writing process. Use the rubrics in this unit to assess your writing.

Personal Narrative	Eyewitness Account
• my most interesting science experiment or project • a scientific or nature discovery of my own • how I started my rock, insect, or other kind of collection	• a fireworks display • a hot-air balloon or air show • a tornado or hurricane • an eclipse

portfolio

School–Home Connection

Keep a writing portfolio. Think about adding the activities from the *Practice the Strategy Notebook* to your writing portfolio. You may want to take your portfolio home to share.

DESCRIPTIVE writing

describes something to the reader.

1
Descriptive Essay

2
Observation Report

DESCRIPTIVE writing

Descriptive Essay

In this chapter, you will practice one kind of descriptive writing: the **descriptive essay**.

In a **descriptive essay,** the writer gives a clear, detailed picture of a specific person, place, or thing.

The story on the next page is a descriptive essay. Study the following questions. Then read the descriptive essay, keeping the questions in mind.

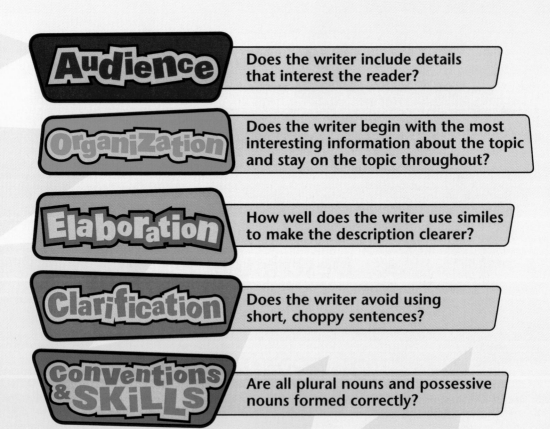

Audience — Does the writer include details that interest the reader?

Organization — Does the writer begin with the most interesting information about the topic and stay on the topic throughout?

Elaboration — How well does the writer use similes to make the description clearer?

Clarification — Does the writer avoid using short, choppy sentences?

Conventions & Skills — Are all plural nouns and possessive nouns formed correctly?

Sarah the Sound Engineer
by David Morrow

Every weekday morning, Sarah and Tex take a taxi to her job. Sarah is a sound engineer for a radio reading service. She happens to be blind. Tex is her guide dog. Radio reading service is for people who are blind or visually impaired. Each day, the service broadcasts articles from newspapers, chapters of books, and interviews. In this way, people who cannot see can receive the same information as sighted people.

At work, Sarah wears headphones and sits at a control desk. In front of her is a panel with small sliding knobs called faders. Faders control the sound that comes from the microphones and the CD and tape players. Sarah has memorized the positions and functions of all the knobs on her panel. Her hands move like lightning across the panel. She quickly adjusts the faders as she listens to the different sounds coming through her headphones. She makes sure that every sound is clear. Her supervisor says Sarah is one of the best sound engineers the reading service has ever had.

Sarah likes her job because she spends the day listening to interesting information and music. Tex likes Sarah's job because the floor underneath her desk is as cool as a cave.

When Sarah gets home from work each day, she takes off her sunglasses and lets her long auburn hair out of its barrette. It flows like a waterfall over her shoulders. Then she puts on her favorite outfit: jeans and a T-shirt. She has trouble finding jeans that are short enough. She is only 5 feet, 1 inch tall, as short as a minute, her father says.

After changing clothes, Sarah turns on classical music, waters her plants, listens to phone messages, returns calls, and cooks dinner. In the evening, she often visits with friends or her sister Meg, who lives in the same town. Sarah and Meg go out to eat at least once a week, usually at their favorite Mexican restaurant.

Sometimes Sarah just stays home and reads. She uses a computer and a scanner. The scanner transmits words from printed pages to the computer, and then the computer reads the words aloud, just like a person. Sarah also has a small computer called Braille'n Speak. It has buttons for the braille alphabet, the raised dots that blind people touch to read. Sarah uses this machine to type in braille or to turn braille dots into printed words. It can read for her, too. Like Tex, both of these machines help Sarah "see."

While Sarah reads, Tex usually sleeps. A large black Labrador retriever, he has been trained to help her. Tex seems as smart as most people. Absolutely nothing escapes his attention. When he is working, he always wears a harness that Sarah holds in her left hand. He watches traffic, pauses at steps, and understands Sarah's commands.

You can see Sarah and Tex all around town. They get on buses, cross busy streets, ride elevators, and sometimes buy lunch at a vendor's stand. They go to restaurants, ice cream shops, concerts, and friends' homes. It's hard to talk about Sarah without talking about Tex. They are a team.

Sarah's life is a lot like most people's lives, but she is different in one way. She never travels alone. She always has the help of a friend named Tex.

Using a Rubric

A rubric is a good way to assess a piece of writing. Rubrics are easy to use. You simply assign 1, 2, 3, or 4 points in each category in the rubric.

Remember the questions you studied on page 58? Those questions were used to make the rubric you see here.

> Hi! My name is Joseph. I'm learning how to write a descriptive essay, too. What did you think about the story on pages 59–61? Let's use this rubric to figure out how well the essay was written. Review the questions in each category in the rubric. Next, read the scoring information for each category. Then, on pages 64–66, you will use this rubric to evaluate the essay.

Audience

Does the writer include details that interest the reader?

Organization

Does the writer begin with the most interesting information about the topic and stay on the topic throughout?

Elaboration

How well does the writer use similes to make the description clearer?

Clarification

Does the writer avoid using short, choppy sentences?

Conventions & Skills

Are all plural nouns and possessive nouns formed correctly?

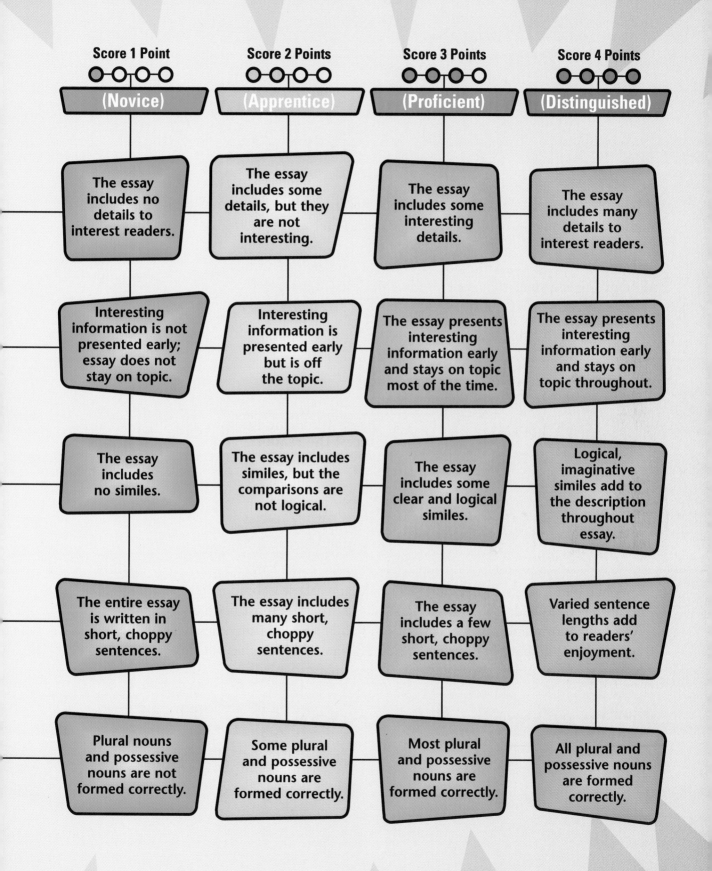

Score 1 Point
(Novice)

The essay includes no details to interest readers.

Interesting information is not presented early; essay does not stay on topic.

The essay includes no similes.

The entire essay is written in short, choppy sentences.

Plural nouns and possessive nouns are not formed correctly.

Score 2 Points
(Apprentice)

The essay includes some details, but they are not interesting.

Interesting information is presented early but is off the topic.

The essay includes similes, but the comparisons are not logical.

The essay includes many short, choppy sentences.

Some plural and possessive nouns are formed correctly.

Score 3 Points
(Proficient)

The essay includes some interesting details.

The essay presents interesting information early and stays on topic most of the time.

The essay includes some clear and logical similes.

The essay includes a few short, choppy sentences.

Most plural and possessive nouns are formed correctly.

Score 4 Points
(Distinguished)

The essay includes many details to interest readers.

The essay presents interesting information early and stays on topic throughout.

Logical, imaginative similes add to the description throughout essay.

Varied sentence lengths add to readers' enjoyment.

All plural and possessive nouns are formed correctly.

Using a Rubric
to Study the Model

Use the rubric to evaluate David's story about Sarah. Remember, you will give 1, 2, 3, or 4 points in each category.

How many points did you give David's story? Discuss each category on the rubric with your classmates. Find words and sentences in the story that support your decision. Then read Joseph's assessment of the story.

Does the writer include details that interest the reader?

> I wondered what kind of dog Tex was and how he helped Sarah—and the writer told me.

While Sarah reads, Tex usually sleeps. A large black Labrador retriever, he has been trained to help her. Tex seems as smart as most people. Absolutely nothing escapes his attention. When he is working, he always wears a harness that Sarah holds in her left hand. He watches traffic, pauses at steps, and understands Sarah's commands.

> The writer grabbed my interest right away by telling me that Sarah was blind. I wanted to know how she could do her job, so I kept reading. I also noticed that every paragraph in the essay was about Sarah or Tex. The writer really did stay on the topic!

Every weekday morning, Sarah and Tex take a taxi to her job. Sarah is a sound engineer for a radio reading service. She happens to be blind. Tex is her guide dog. Radio reading service is for people who are blind or visually impaired. Each day, the service broadcasts articles from newspapers, chapters of books, and interviews. In this way, people who cannot see can receive the same information as sighted people.

How well does the writer use similes to make the description clearer?

> This writer used several similes to describe Sarah. His comparisons helped me picture how her hair looks as it falls over her shoulders. The simile 'as short as a minute' made me smile.

When Sarah gets home from work each day, she takes off her sunglasses and lets her long auburn hair out of its barrette. It flows like a waterfall over her shoulders. Then she puts on her favorite outfit: jeans and a T-shirt. She has trouble finding jeans that are short enough. She is only 5 feet, 1 inch tall, as short as a minute, her father says.

Clarification — Does the writer avoid using short, choppy sentences?

> I could see where the writer combined short sentences to make the essay easier to read. For example, what if he had written 'After changing clothes, Sarah turns on classical music. Then she waters her plants. Next, she listens to phone messages. After that, she returns calls.' Combining all those thoughts into one sentence made the essay much more interesting, didn't it?

After changing clothes, Sarah turns on classical music, waters her plants, listens to phone messages, returns calls, and cooks dinner. In the evening, she often visits with friends or her sister Meg, who lives in the same town. Sarah and Meg go out to eat at least once a week, usually at their favorite Mexican restaurant.

Conventions & SKILLS — Are all plural nouns and possessive nouns formed correctly?

> Yes, this writer used the correct form of plural and possessive nouns. When I reread the essay, I found **buses,** (a plural noun with tricky spelling), **vendor's** (a singular possessive noun), **friends'** (a plural possessive noun), and **people's** (another plural possessive noun).

" Now it's my turn to write!

I'm going to write my own descriptive essay. Follow along, and you will see how I use good writing strategies. I will also use the model essay and the rubric to guide my writing. "

JoSePh

Writer of a Descriptive Essay

Name: Joseph
Home: New York City
Hobbies: lacrosse; learning about Native Americans; writing e-mail
Favorite Book: *Bearstone* by Will Hobbs
Hero: my great-grandfather
Assignment: descriptive essay

Prewriting

Gather

Think about people who interest me. Gather information about their personalities, appearance, and interests.

> My family is Native American, and I like to learn about our customs and culture. My great-grandfather has taught me most of what I know about the Mohawk side of our family. He was a construction worker in New York City when he was young. He helped build the Empire State Building.
>
> "When my teacher asked us to write descriptive essays, I didn't have to think too long before I came up with my topic. My great-grandfather, Joseph Cloud, is the most interesting person I know. I'm even named after him. I'm going to write my descriptive essay about him."

Notes About Joseph Cloud

- is my great-grandfather
- wants to preserve Mohawk heritage
- shares his hopes and dreams with me
- tells great stories
- is a good teacher
- taught me about stars
- taught me about lacrosse and snow snake
- taught me about my forefathers
- is the reason my family lives in Brooklyn
- moved to NYC when he was young
- became an ironworker
- helped build Empire State Building
- speaks and teaches the Mohawk language

Go to page 28 in the **Practice** the Strategy **Notebook!**

Prewriting

Organize

Use my notes to make a spider map.

"I know from the **Rubric** that organization is important. I decided to make a spider map to help organize my thoughts."

Spider Map

A **spider map** organizes information about a topic. The topic is written in the center. Important details are written on the "legs."

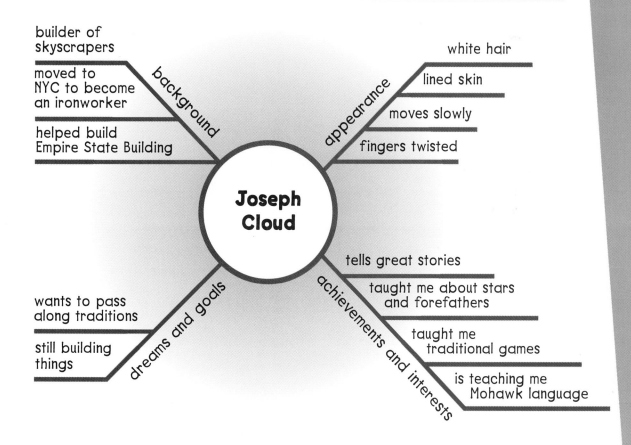

background
- builder of skyscrapers
- moved to NYC to become an ironworker
- helped build Empire State Building

appearance
- white hair
- lined skin
- moves slowly
- fingers twisted

Joseph Cloud

dreams and goals
- wants to pass along traditions
- still building things

achievements and interests
- tells great stories
- taught me about stars and forefathers
- taught me traditional games
- is teaching me Mohawk language

Go to page 30 in the **Practice the Strategy Notebook!**

Drafting

Write

Draft my description. Begin by describing the most interesting thing about my topic.

"Now I'm ready to write! First, I need to choose the most interesting thing about my great-grandfather. Lots of things about him interest me, but I have to think about my audience. It will be my classmates. I think they will be interested in the fact that my great-grandfather helped build the Empire State Building. I'll start with that! You can read my first paragraph on the next page."

Joseph Clouds journey began in 1928. He was nineteen years old and living in upstate New York. Like many Mohawk mens, he knew that he could earn better wages working in construction. By the Fall of 1930, he was working on one of New York Cities' grandist projects. It was the construction of the Empire State Building. Like other **most interesting** Mohawk ironworkers, Joseph Cloud was not afraid of heights. **thing** He was sure-footed on the dangerous steel girders. He and other Mohawks helped build many of the skyscraper's along the east coast. Many of them settled in New York City. They lived in brooklyn. Joseph Cloud did.

> 66 As I write the rest of my essay, I want my class-mates to be able to picture my great-grandfather, as if he is standing right in front of them. I will write detailed descriptions about what he looks like, what kind of person he is, and what his life has been like. I won't worry about making mistakes in spelling or grammar right now. I will just do my best and check for mistakes later. 99

Go to page 32 in the **Practice** the Strategy **Notebook!**

Elaborate
Add similes to make my description clearer.

66 When I reread my first draft, I wondered what I could do to make my descriptions better. Then I remembered from the **Rubric** that using similes would make my descriptions clearer.

"That's a good idea! Still, I don't want to use boring similes like 'his hair is as white as snow.' I'll try to think of more interesting comparisons to help my audience clearly picture my great-grandfather. 99

Simile

A **simile** compares two different things by using the word *like* or *as*. Here is a simile that compares a man and a cat:

Joseph Cloud was as sure-footed as a **cat**.

[2nd DRAFT]

similes

My great-grandfather doesn't move as quickly as he used to. He is

an old man now. His hair is long and white, and he pulls it away from
                              ∧ as as chalk   ∧ like the branches of an old
his deeply lined face with a piece of leather. His fingers are gnarled,
oak tree   ∧

and they often rest upon a wooden cane. There is one thing about

him that still seems young. It is his eyes. They are bright and alert.

Joseph Cloud has seen many things in his long life, and he has lots

of stories and wisdom to share. His voice rumbles whenever
                                         like thunder ← simile
                                    ∧

he speaks.

Go to page 34 in the **Practice** the Strategy **Notebook!**
                                  ∧

Revising

Clarify   Combine short, choppy sentences.

"When I read my essay to Karin, my partner, she said that there were too many short and choppy sentences. She was right. My writing didn't flow smoothly.

"After I combined some of my short, choppy sentences, they sounded much better."

READ TO
A PARTNER

Short, Choppy Sentence

Short, choppy sentences make writing hard to read. Pairs of short sentences on the same topic should be combined.
Short and choppy: Joseph Cloud is an elder. He is in the Mohawk community.
Better: Joseph Cloud is an elder in the Mohawk community.

---

combined sentences

[3rd DRAFT]

Joseph's ~~last name is~~ Cloud. ~~He~~ is my teacher. Almost everything I know about my Mohawk heritage, I have learned from him. He teaches me storys of my forefathers. ~~He teaches me~~ legends about the stars in the night sky ,and ~~He teaches me~~ traditional games like lacrosse. He also teaches me the Mohawk language.

Go to page 35 in the **Practice** the Strategy **Notebook!**

Editing

Proofread

Check to see that plural nouns and possessive nouns are formed correctly.

> Now I need to proofread my work. I will check my spelling, capitalization, and punctuation, of course. I will also make sure I used the correct form of plural nouns and possessive nouns. You can see some of the mistakes I found and fixed on the next page.

Plural and Possessive Nouns

Plural Nouns

Add -*s* or -*es* to form the plural of most nouns.

Examples: voice ⟶ voices; dish ⟶ dish**es**

Change *y* to *i* and add -*es* to form the plural of some nouns ending in *y*.

Example: sky ⟶ sk**ies**

Change *f* to *v* and add -*es* to form the plural of some nouns ending in *f*.

Example: leaf ⟶ lea**ves**

Some nouns change their spelling or remain unchanged in their plural form.

Examples: man ⟶ men; sheep ⟶ sheep

Possessive Nouns

Add an **apostrophe** and -*s* to form the possessive of singular and plural nouns that do not end in *s*.

Examples: the man's face; the men's faces

Add only an apostrophe to form the possessive of plural nouns that end in *s*.

Example: the workers' boots

Extra Practice

See **Plural and Possessive Nouns** (pages CS 6–CS 7) in the back of this book.

Descriptive Writing • Descriptive Essay

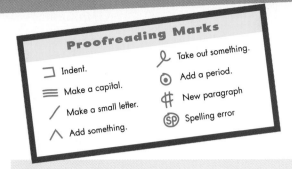

Still Building

[4th DRAFT]

possessive noun

Joseph Clouds journey began in 1928. He was nineteen years old

and living in upstate New York. Like many Mohawk mens, he knew   plural noun

that he could earn better wages working in construction. By the fall

possessive noun ⟶ City's (SP) grandest

of 1930, he was working on one of New York Cities grandist proj-

ects. It was the construction of the Empire State Building. Like other

Mohawk ironworkers, Joseph Cloud was not afraid of heights. He

was as sure-footed as a cat on the dangerous steel girders. He and

other Mohawks helped build many of the skyscrapers along the   plural noun

plural noun ⟶

East Coast. Many Mohawks settled in a section of New York City

plural noun ⟶ (SP) families   (SP) there.

named brooklyn. Many Mohawk familys, including mine, still live their.

⌗ Joseph Cloud is my teacher. Almost everything I know about my

(SP) stories

Mohawk heritage, I have learned from him. He teaches me storys of   plural

(SP) skies   nouns

my forefathers, legends about the stars in the night skys, and tradi-

tional games like lacrosse. He also teaches me the Mohawk language.

He always says, "When no person of our nation speaks our language,

we will no longer exist." Joseph Cloud wants to be sure that I will

be able to pass along our Mohawk traditions.

the Strategy

Go to page 36 in the **Practice** ∧ **Notebook!**

Publishing

Share
Publish my descriptive essay in a class newsletter.

> **Writer:** Joseph
> **Assignment:** descriptive essay
> **Topic:** my great-grandfather
> **Audience:** classmates
> **Method of Publication:** publish in the class newsletter
> **Reason for Choice:** to tell my readers about an interesting person

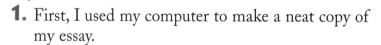

We publish a class newsletter every month. In each issue, we include a feature on an interesting person. I submitted my descriptive essay on my great-grandfather because I think that my classmates will enjoy reading about him.

"I was excited when our editorial committee selected my essay. When my essay was published, I got extra copies and gave them to all my relatives. Everyone enjoyed my descriptive essay, especially my great-grandfather!

"Here are the steps I followed to submit my work.

1. First, I used my computer to make a neat copy of my essay.

2. I wrote a letter to the editorial committee explaining why I would like to see the essay published.

3. I put the letter and essay in an envelope and put it in the submission box for our class newsletter.

Still Building
by Joseph

Joseph Cloud's journey began in 1928. He was nineteen years old and living in upstate New York. Like many Mohawk men, he knew that he could earn better wages working in construction. By the fall of 1930, he was working on one of New York City's grandest projects. It was the construction of the Empire State Building. Like other Mohawk ironworkers, Joseph Cloud was not afraid of heights. He was as sure-footed as a cat on the dangerous steel girders. He and other Mohawks helped build many of the skyscrapers along the East Coast. Many Mohawks settled in a section of New York City named Brooklyn. Many Mohawk families, including mine, still live there.

Joseph Cloud is my teacher. Almost everything I know about my Mohawk heritage, I have learned from him. He teaches me stories of my forefathers, legends about the stars in the night skies, and traditional games like lacrosse. He also teaches me the Mohawk language. He always says, "When no person of our nation speaks our language, we will no longer exist." Joseph Cloud wants to be sure that I will be able to pass along our Mohawk traditions.

This man is an elder in the Mohawk community. He is also my great-grandfather. He is the reason my family lives in New York City, and the story of his move from the reservation to the city is one of my favorites.

My great-grandfather doesn't move as quickly as he used to. He is an old man now. His hair is long and as white as chalk, and he pulls it away from his deeply lined face with a piece of leather. His fingers are gnarled like the branches of an old oak tree, and they often rest upon a wooden cane. There is one thing about him that still seems young. It is his eyes. They are bright and alert.

Joseph Cloud has seen many things in his long life, and he has lots of stories and wisdom to share. His voice rumbles like thunder whenever he speaks. He urges us to preserve our heritage. He tells us about his hopes for the Mohawk and our way of life. He says that he is still a construction worker, but now he is helping to build our future. We are all lucky to have Joseph Cloud in our lives, especially me!

USING the Rubric for Assessment

Go to page 38 in the **Practice the Strategy Notebook!** Use that rubric to assess Joseph's paper. Try using the rubric to assess your own writing.

DESCRIPTIVE writing

Observation Report

In this chapter, you will practice another kind of descriptive writing: the **observation report**.

In an **observation report,** the writer describes in detail an object, person, event, or process. An observation report is similar to an eyewitness account, but the emphasis is more on describing something rather than telling a story. Observations are often kept in journals as records.

The journal entry on the next page is an observation report. Study the following questions. Then read the observation report, keeping the questions in mind.

 **Audience** — Has the writer chosen important details that will inform the reader?

 **Organization** — Are the paragraphs organized with a topic sentence followed by supporting details?

 **Elaboration** — Is the description complete?

 **Clarification** — Do the sentences begin in a variety of ways?

 **Conventions & Skills** — Do all the subjects and verbs agree?

New Mexico Piñon Pines
November 25
by Evan Burns

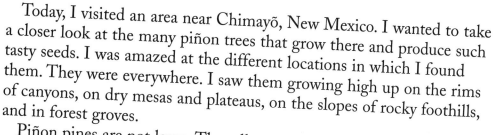

Today, I visited an area near Chimayõ, New Mexico. I wanted to take a closer look at the many piñon trees that grow there and produce such tasty seeds. I was amazed at the different locations in which I found them. They were everywhere. I saw them growing high up on the rims of canyons, on dry mesas and plateaus, on the slopes of rocky foothills, and in forest groves.

Piñon pines are not large. The tallest one I saw was about 35 feet high, about as tall as a three-story building. The trunks are only one to two feet in diameter, and most of the trunks are crooked and irregular. Reddish branches reach up to form a rounded top on many piñon pines. Sprouting from these branches are short pine needles that grow in pairs. They give off a wonderful evergreen scent. Nestled within the needles are small, egg-shaped pinecones. The largest ones I saw were only two inches long. The pinecones are yellowish-brown, and a sticky resin covered my hands after I touched them.

Piñon pinecones contain large seeds. These seeds are the sweet, rich piñon nuts, or pine nuts, that I like to eat. When the pinecone opens up, the piñon seeds fall out. Walking among the trees, I talked to some people who were harvesting the seeds. Proudly, they showed me burlap bags stuffed with piñon seeds. In one year, a single piñon pine can produce nine bushels of seeds!

People are not the only creatures who enjoy eating piñon nuts. I spotted jays, quails, and wild turkeys eating every seed they could find. I've heard that bears and deer eat piñon seeds, too, but I didn't see any today. I did, however, see porcupines and many wood rats. I noticed that one wood rat ran into a hole in a tree. After he left, I looked inside and saw a stash of seeds that he had put away for the winter.

When I returned to the city this evening and had dinner, there were delicious piñon nuts on my salad. I thought about these trees that can grow out of rock, endure the wind and heat, survive dry conditions, and provide food for both humans and animals. They are truly a wonder!

Using a Rubric

A rubric is a good way to assess a piece of writing. Rubrics are easy to use. You simply assign 1, 2, 3, or 4 points in each category in the rubric.

Remember the questions that you studied on page 78? Those questions were used to make the rubric you see here.

"Hi! My name is Rebecca. I'm learning how to write an observation report, too. What did you think about the report on page 79? Let's use this rubric to figure out how well the report was written. Review the questions in each category in the rubric. Next, read the scoring information for each category. On pages 82–84, you will use this rubric to evaluate the report."

Audience

Has the writer chosen important details that will inform the reader?

Organization

Are the paragraphs organized with a topic sentence followed by supporting details?

Elaboration

Is the description complete?

Clarification

Do the sentences begin in a variety of ways?

Conventions & Skills

Do all the subjects and verbs agree?

Descriptive Writing • Observation Report

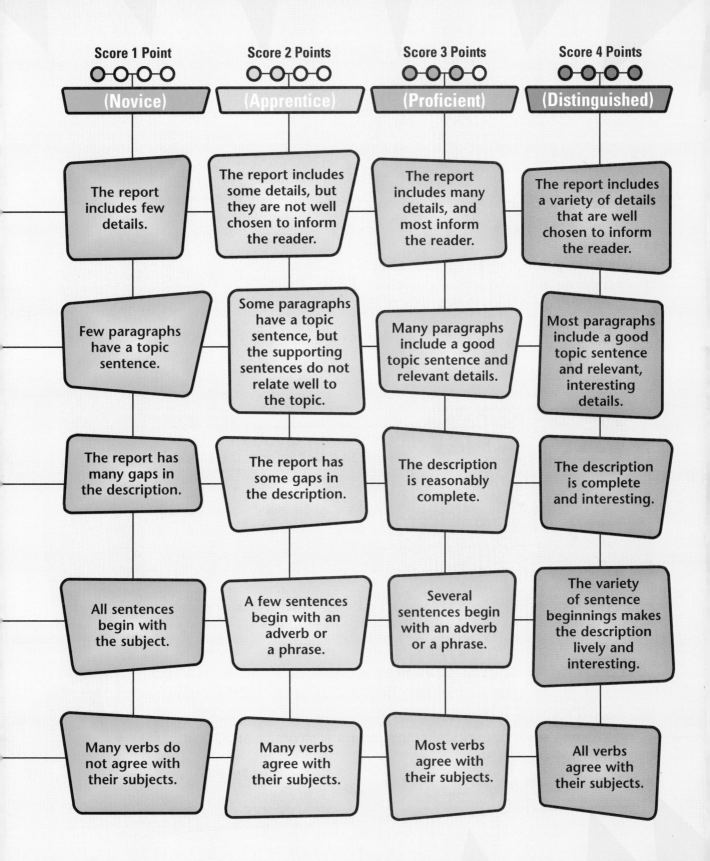

Score 1 Point	Score 2 Points	Score 3 Points	Score 4 Points
(Novice)	**(Apprentice)**	**(Proficient)**	**(Distinguished)**
The report includes few details.	The report includes some details, but they are not well chosen to inform the reader.	The report includes many details, and most inform the reader.	The report includes a variety of details that are well chosen to inform the reader.
Few paragraphs have a topic sentence.	Some paragraphs have a topic sentence, but the supporting sentences do not relate well to the topic.	Many paragraphs include a good topic sentence and relevant details.	Most paragraphs include a good topic sentence and relevant, interesting details.
The report has many gaps in the description.	The report has some gaps in the description.	The description is reasonably complete.	The description is complete and interesting.
All sentences begin with the subject.	A few sentences begin with an adverb or a phrase.	Several sentences begin with an adverb or a phrase.	The variety of sentence beginnings makes the description lively and interesting.
Many verbs do not agree with their subjects.	Many verbs agree with their subjects.	Most verbs agree with their subjects.	All verbs agree with their subjects.

Using a Rubric

to Study the Model

Use the rubric to evaluate Evan's observation report. Remember, you will give a score of 1, 2, 3, or 4 points in each category.

How many points did you give Evan's report? Discuss each category on the rubric with your classmates. Find words and sentences in the report that support your decisions. Then read Rebecca's assessment of the report.

Has the writer chosen important details that will inform the reader?

66 In the first paragraph, the writer doesn't just write that these trees can live where it's dry and rocky. He provides important details so that I can understand all the places where the trees grow. 99

Today, I visited an area near Chimayō, New Mexico. I wanted to take a closer look at the many piñon trees that grow there and produce such tasty seeds. I was amazed at the different locations in which I found them. They were everywhere. I saw them growing high up on the rims of canyons, on dry mesas and plateaus, on the slopes of rocky foothills, and in forest groves.

Organization

Are the paragraphs organized with a topic sentence followed by supporting details?

"The writer begins each paragraph in his report with a topic sentence, and then he adds details. See how he starts this paragraph? I know right away that it's going to tell about creatures that eat piñon nuts."

People are not the only creatures who enjoy eating piñon nuts. I spotted jays, quails, and wild turkeys eating every seed they could find. I've heard that bears and deer eat piñon seeds, too, but I didn't see any today. I did, however, see porcupines and many wood rats. I noticed that one wood rat ran into a hole in a tree. After he left, I looked inside and saw a stash of seeds that he had put away for the winter.

Elaboration

Is the description complete?

"The writer added a lot of details about the trees. He helped me see, smell, and feel what they're like. He even helped me picture how tall 35 feet is!"

Piñon pines are not large. The tallest one I saw was about 35 feet high, about as tall as a three-story building. The trunks are only one to two feet in diameter, and most of the trunks are crooked and irregular. Reddish branches reach up to form a rounded top on many piñon pines. Sprouting from these branches are short pine needles that grow in pairs. They give off a wonderful evergreen scent. Nestled within the needles are small, egg-shaped pinecones. The largest ones I saw were only two inches long. The pinecones are yellowish-brown, and a sticky resin covered my hands after I touched them.

Clarification — Do the sentences begin in a variety of ways?

"The writer began some sentences with the subject, of course. However, he made this description much more interesting by starting other sentences with adverbs and phrases, such as **Proudly, Walking among the trees,** and **In one year.**"

Walking among the trees, I talked to some people who were harvesting the seeds. Proudly, they showed me burlap bags stuffed with piñon seeds. In one year, a single piñon pine can produce nine bushels of seeds!

Conventions & Skills — Do all the subjects and verbs agree?

Yes, the writer made sure that each verb agrees with its subject. The sentence below was especially tricky. It would have been easier if the words had been in the usual order: 'Small, egg-shaped **pinecones are** nestled within the needles.' Still, variety makes writing more interesting!

Nestled within the needles are small, egg-shaped pinecones.

" Now it's my turn to write!

I'm going to write my own observation report. Follow along, and you will see how I use good writing strategies. I will also use the model report and the rubric to guide my writing. "

Rebecca

Writer of an Observation Report

Name:	Rebecca
Home:	Mississippi
Hobbies:	camping, hiking, writing in my journal
Favorite Clothes:	jeans my aunt gave me for my last birthday
Favorite Book:	*Dear Mr. Henshaw* by Beverly Cleary
Assignment:	observation report

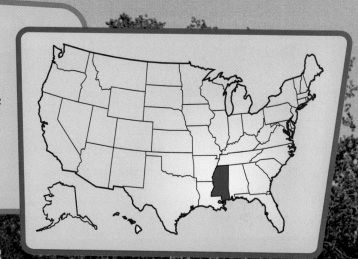

Prewriting

Gather
Take notes on what I am observing.

❝ Right before our spring break, my teacher told us we were going to write an observation report. He asked us to take notes on something we observed while we were on break. My family was going to visit Grandma during the break. She lives near the Atlantic coast on a really interesting salt marsh. Salt water flows in and out with the tide, and all kinds of plants and animals live there.

"I decided to take notes on the salt marsh. I also sketched what I saw. Later, I used a field guide to help identify some of the things I saw. Here are my notes: ❞

high and low tides
salt water
herons and egrets in marsh
birds eat -   snails
              fiddler crabs
              fish
insects -   no-see-ums
              mosquitoes
              deer flies
sounds -   crickets
              frogs
              birds
spartina grass
cattails
algae
strong smell
shrubs along the edge

Go to page 40 in the **Practice the Strategy Notebook!**

Prewriting

Organize

Organize my notes into a network tree.

66 I know from the **Rubric** that organization is important. After I studied my notes, I decided to make a network tree. A network tree can help me organize my thoughts. 99

Network Tree

A **network tree** organizes information. The topic goes at the top, and main points about the topic go on the next level. Details about each main point go on the bottom.

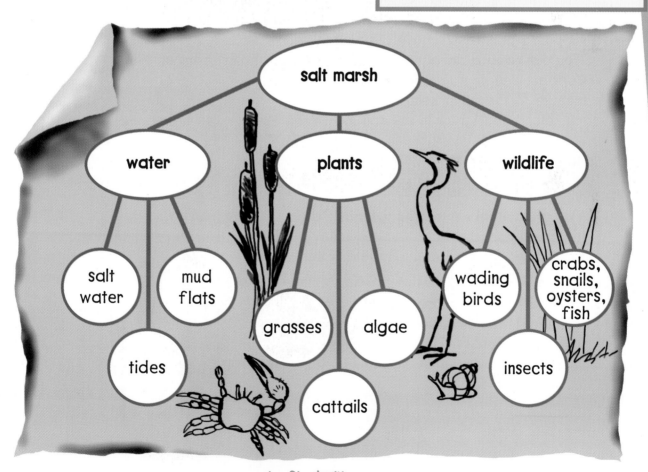

Go to page 42 in the **Practice** the Strategy **Notebook!**

Drafting

Write
Draft my report. For each main point in my network tree, write a topic sentence and add details.

"Now I'll use my network tree to organize my report. I will write a topic sentence for each main point and then add more sentences with details from my tree.

"The **Rubric** reminds me to choose details that will inform my audience. This time, I am my own audience! When I read my observation report many years from now, I want to remember how the salt marsh looked, smelled, and felt. Good, clear descriptions will help me do that. I'll also share my report with my classmates, so I will keep them in mind as I decide which details to include.

"You can read a paragraph from my observation report on the next page. See how I started with a topic sentence? All the other sentences are details about plants that grow in the salt marsh."

Topic Sentence, Detail Sentence

A **topic sentence** states the main idea of the paragraph. It is often the first sentence, but it may be placed in the middle or at the end of the paragraph.

A **detail sentence** supports the paragraph's main idea. The detail sentences in each paragraph should tell about the main idea.

— topic sentence

The moist salt marsh is a perfect area for plants to grow.

Cordgrass gives the marsh its yellowish-green color. It stands five

or six feet tall, and its long thin reeds sway in the breeze. Black

shorter
needle rush reaches my waist, and the ∧spartina grass comes up to

examine
my knees. As I ~~look at~~ ∧ the standing water and tidal creeks, I can

see colorful saltwater plankton and clumps of algae floating on the

Both are blooming, and they make the water thick and soupy.
surface. ∧Along the edges of the marsh are cattails and shrubs. Salt

myrtle and marsh elder are two shrubs I can identify.

detail
sentences

Go to page 44 in the **Practice** the Strategy ∧ **Notebook!**

Revising

Elaborate

Fill in any gaps in my description.

❝ When I reread my first draft, some of the descriptions still didn't seem complete. The **Rubric** mentioned that I should fill in any gaps in my description, so I decided to add more details.

"For example, I had mentioned the wading birds, but I didn't tell what they looked like. If I write more complete descriptions, I will be better able to recall all the interesting things I observed in my grandmother's salt marsh. ❞

[2nd DRAFT]

A great blue heron not far from me are nearly four feet tall and has bent its long neck into an "S" shape. Smaller blue herons and white egrets circle overhead and lands in the marsh.

Although the tall grasses makes it hard to see, the salt marsh is full of wildlife. The first things I notice are the large wading birds. Other birds stand quietly as they scan the water and the mud flats for food. The wading birds also eat insects. Looking more closely, I see grasshoppers, deer flies, and dragonflies. Although I can't see them, I know the "no-see-ums" is out. They keep biting my arms and legs.

They search for crabs, snails, oysters, clams, and small fish. These smaller creatures live in the mud flats, on plants, or in the salty marsh waters.

Go to page 46 in the **Practice** the Strategy **Notebook!**

Revising

Clarify
Make sure my sentences begin in a variety of ways.

> By now, my observation report included all my main ideas and the important details, but I still wasn't satisfied. It just didn't sound right.
>
> "Here's where the **Rubric** helped me again. It reminded me to start my sentences in different ways to add interest to my report. When I checked, I discovered that nearly all my sentences began with the subject. That can get boring! I will try starting some sentences with phrases or with adverbs. In fact, some phrases really are adverbs. What do you think of my changes?

[3rd DRAFT]

adverb   The salt marsh is a tidal wetland that connects the ocean and the land. Twice daily, the tide floods in and out of it. Now the tide is low. Throughout the morning, water has been draining out of the marsh and back into the ocean. Soggy mud flats stand where tidal water has been, and a small tidal creek glistens as it snakes out of sight. Damp and mushy, the ground sucks at my shoes wherever I step.

adverb

phrase

phrase

Go to page 47 in the **Practice the Strategy Notebook!**

Editing

Proofread
Check to see that all subjects and verbs agree.

> Now I need to proofread my report. I always check my spelling, capitalization, and punctuation. Today, I will also check to see that the verb in each sentence agrees with its subject. You can see some of the mistakes I corrected in the paragraphs on the next page.

Subject-Verb Agreement

- **Verbs With Singular Subjects**

  Add **-s** or **-es** to a verb when the subject is singular.

  Example: The high **tide floods** the marsh.

- **Verbs With Plural Subjects**

  Do not add **-s** or **-es** when the subject is a plural or is one of the pronouns *I, you, we,* or *they.*

  Examples: Birds wade in the marsh. **I love** to watch them.

- **Using Forms of the Verb "to be"**

  Use *am* after *I.*

  Example: I am amazed by the sound of the crickets and birds.

  Use *is* or *was* after singular subjects.

  Example: The **sound is** pleasant and musical.

  Use *are* or *were* with plural subjects.

  Example: Salt **marshes are** full of life.

Extra Practice
See **Subject-Verb Agreement** (pages CS 8–CS 9) in the back of this book.

[4th DRAFT]

plural subject and verb

Although the tall grasses makes it hard to see, the salt marsh is
full of wildlife. The first things I notice are the large wading birds.

is ← singular subject and verb

A great blue heron not far from me are nearly four feet tall and has
bent its long neck into an "S" shape. Smaller blue herons and white

plural subject and verb

egrets circle overhead and lands in the marsh. Other birds stand
quietly as they scan the water and mud flats for food. They search

fiddler

for crabs, snails, oysters, clams, and small fish. These smaller creatures all live in the mud flats, on plants, or in the salty marsh waters.
The wading birds also eat insects. Looking more closely, I see
grasshoppers, deer flies, and dragonflies. Although I can't see them,

are

I know the "no-see-ums" is out. They keep biting my arms and legs.

plural
subject
and verb

This salt marsh is a good example of the ecosystems I learned
about in school. The tidal waters, the mud, the plants, and the

S ←

wildlife all works together. Each part depend upon the other parts.

S

I am glad that my grandmother live here and that I get to visit her
often. I can't wait to explore this salt marsh again!

singular
subject and
verb

the Strategy
Go to page 48 in the **Practice Notebook!**

Publishing

Share
Record my report in an observation journal.

Writer:	Rebecca
Assignment:	observation report
Topic:	salt marsh
Audience:	my classmates and me
Method of Publication:	record my report in an observation journal and put it on display
Reason for Choice:	to help me recall and share things I have observed

"I like the idea of keeping an observation journal. I can record descriptions of interesting things that I see. Then I can refresh my memory by rereading what I have written.
   "This is how I created my report and shared it in an observation journal."

1. I wrote the location and date of my observation at the beginning of the entry.

2. Next, I recorded my observations.

3. I illustrated my report with drawings and some photographs. I drew a grassy backgound for my report, too.

4. I displayed the pages from my observation journal by propping them up on a bookstand.

The Salt Marsh Behind Grandma's House

April 15
by Rebecca

The salt marsh I am exploring is behind my grandmother's house in Georgia, near the coast of the Atlantic Ocean. The marsh stretches as far as my eyes can see. As I step into the marsh, the sun is high, and a warm, humid stickiness surrounds me. I take a deep breath and inhale the strong, murky smell of salt water, lush green plants, and muddy decay. The air is filled with the sounds of insects and birds, a sound my grandma calls "marsh music." Walking into the salt marsh is like entering a different world.

The salt marsh is a tidal wetland that connects the ocean and the land. Twice daily, the tide floods in and out of it. Now the tide is low. Throughout the morning, salt water has been draining out of the marsh and back into the ocean. Soggy mud flats stand where tidal water has been, and a small tidal creek glistens as it snakes out of sight. The tidal creek is there only at low tide. At high tide, that whole area is under water. Damp and mushy, the ground sucks at my shoes wherever I step.

The moist salt marsh is a perfect area for plants to grow. Cordgrass gives the marsh its yellowish-green color. It stands five or six feet tall, which is taller than I am. Its long thin reeds sway in the breeze. Black needle rush reaches my waist, and the shorter spartina grass comes up to my knees. As I examine the standing water and tidal creeks, I can see colorful saltwater plankton and clumps of algae floating on the surface. Both are blooming, and they make the water thick and soupy. Along the edges of the marsh are cattails and shrubs. Salt myrtle and marsh elder are two shrubs I can identify.

Although the tall grasses make it hard to see what's here, the salt marsh is full of wildlife. The first things I notice are the large wading birds. A great blue heron not far from me

Descriptive Writing · Observation Report

is nearly four feet tall and has bent its long neck into an "S" shape. Smaller blue herons and white egrets circle overhead and land in the marsh. Other birds stand quietly as they scan the water and mud flats for food. They search for fiddler crabs, snails, oysters, clams, and small fish. These smaller creatures live in the mud flats, on plants, or in the marsh waters. The wading birds also eat insects. Looking more closely, I see grasshoppers, deer flies, and dragonflies. Although I can't see them, I know the "no-see-ums" are out. They keep biting my arms and legs!

This salt marsh is a good example of the ecosystems I learned about in school. The tidal waters, the mud, the plants, and the wildlife all work together. Each part depends on the other parts. These plants could not live here without the saltwater tide every day, and the wildlife would not be here at all if there were no plants. I am glad that my grandmother lives here and that I get to visit her often. I can't wait to explore this salt marsh again!

USING the Rubric for Assessment

Go to page 50 in the **Practice** the Strategy **Notebook!** Use that rubric to assess Rebecca's paper. Try using the rubric to assess your own writing.

your own DESCRIPTIVE writing

Science

Put the strategies you practiced in this unit to work to write your own descriptive essay, observation report, or both! You can:

- develop the writing you did in the Your Own Writing pages of the *Practice the Strategy Notebook*;
- pick an idea below and write something new;
- choose another idea of your own.

Be sure to follow the steps in the writing process. Use the rubrics in this unit to assess your writing.

Descriptive Essay	Observation Report
• a meteorologist who works at a local television station • a cave with stalactites and stalagmites • cirrus, cumulus, or nimbus clouds • a zoo keeper • the effect of a drought	• a science experiment • a chameleon changing colors • tadpoles changing into frogs • amoebas multiplying • an earthquake

portfolio

Keep a writing portfolio. Think about adding the activities from the *Practice the Strategy Notebook* to your writing portfolio. You may want to take your portfolio home to share.

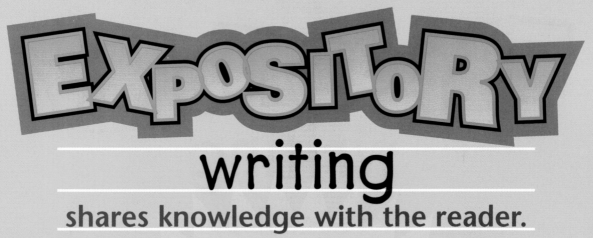

EXPOSITORY writing

shares knowledge with the reader.

1
Research Report

2
Compare-and-Contrast Essay

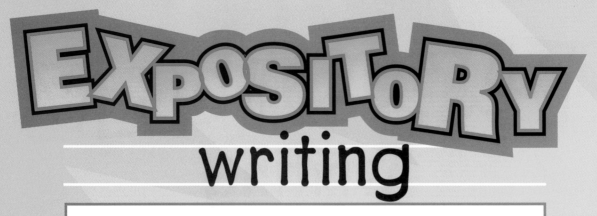

Research Report

In this chapter, you will practice one kind of expository writing: the **research report**.

A **research report** shares information. The writer of a research report must gather information about a topic, organize it in a logical way, and explain to others what he or she has learned.

Study the following questions. Then read the research report on the next page, keeping the questions in mind.

Audience — Does the writer explain words that the audience might not understand?

Organization — Does the writer organize the body of the report so it clearly presents and develops the main points?

Elaboration — Do the introduction and conclusion add to the report by stating the topic and summarizing the main points?

Clarification — Does the writer focus the report by including only necessary information?

Conventions & SKILLS — Does the writer correctly capitalize proper nouns, proper adjectives, and abbreviations?

Chief Joseph
by Matthew Hobbs

Chief Joseph, a Nez Percé, was one of the greatest Native American leaders. There are not many Nez Percé left now. They once lived in the area known today as Idaho, Oregon, and Washington. Peaceful people, they helped explorers who came to their territory in the early 1800s. Later, they accepted the American settlers who lived on their land. Chief Joseph devoted his life to helping and protecting the Nez Percé people.

Chief Joseph's people faced many problems beginning in 1860. That year, gold was discovered in their territory. The U.S. government wanted this land and its valuable resources. It tried to force the Nez Percé to move to a reservation in Idaho. A reservation is land that the government set aside for Native Americans. Chief Joseph tried to preserve his people's right to the land where they had lived for hundreds of years. Finally, he did attempt to move his people to the reservation. However, U.S. troops attacked them along the way, and the Nez Percé War began.

Chief Joseph was a brave and intelligent leader. Under his leadership, the Nez Percé fought and won many battles against the U.S. troops. In time, Chief Joseph and other Nez Percé leaders knew they could not win the war. They decided to lead their people into Canada. There they would be safe from the U.S. troops. However, as they crossed Montana, U.S. troops pursued them. After a five-day battle with many deaths on both sides, the Nez Percé were forced to surrender. The survivors were sent to the Indian Territory of Oklahoma. There, many suffered and died.

Chief Joseph continued to fight for his people. He traveled to Washington, D.C., and spoke to lawmakers there. He told of the suffering of the Nez Percé and convinced the lawmakers to send them back to Idaho. Most of the remaining Nez Percé people still live there today.

Like many great American leaders, Chief Joseph fought for freedom and equality. When he spoke in Washington, he said, "Treat all men alike. Give them all the same law. Give them all an even chance to live and grow." These are still American ideals today.

Using a Rubric

A rubric is a good way to assess a piece of writing. Rubrics are easy to use. You simply assign 1, 2, 3, or 4 points in each category in the rubric.

Remember the questions that you read on page 100? Those questions were used to make the rubric you see here.

" Hi! My name is Selena. I'm learning how to write a research report, too. What did you think of the report on page 101? Let's use this rubric to figure out how well this report was written. Review the questions in each category in the rubric. Next, read the scoring information for each category. Then, on pages 104–106, you and I will use this rubric to assess the report. "

Audience
Does the writer explain words that the audience might not understand?

Organization
Does the writer organize the body of the report so it clearly presents and develops the main points?

Elaboration
Do the introduction and conclusion add to the report by stating the topic and summarizing the main points?

Clarification
Does the writer focus the report by including only necessary information?

Conventions & Skills
Does the writer correctly capitalize proper nouns, proper adjectives, and abbreviations?

Expository Writing • Research Report

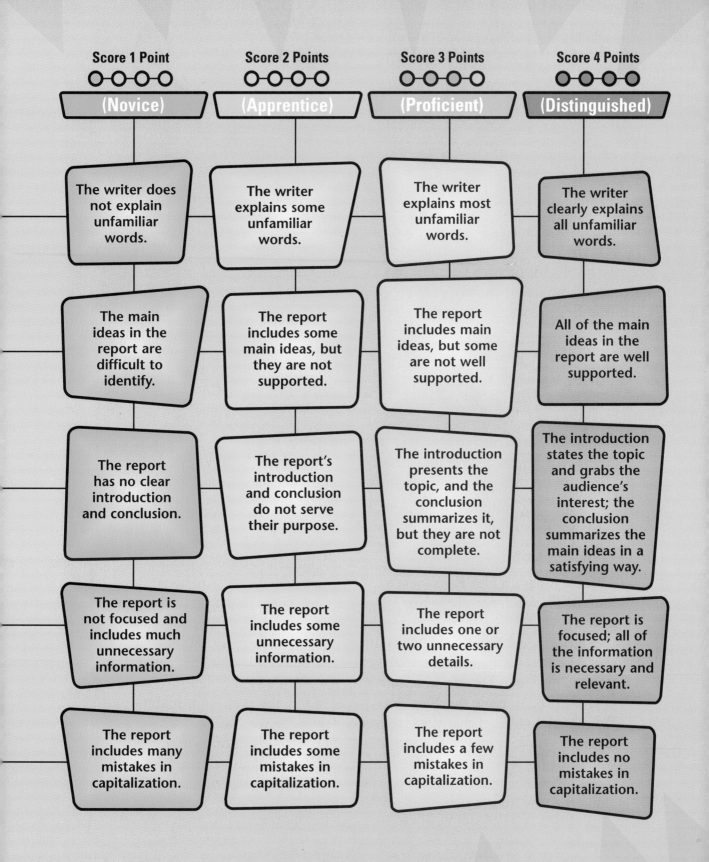

Score 1 Point (Novice)	Score 2 Points (Apprentice)	Score 3 Points (Proficient)	Score 4 Points (Distinguished)
The writer does not explain unfamiliar words.	The writer explains some unfamiliar words.	The writer explains most unfamiliar words.	The writer clearly explains all unfamiliar words.
The main ideas in the report are difficult to identify.	The report includes some main ideas, but they are not supported.	The report includes main ideas, but some are not well supported.	All of the main ideas in the report are well supported.
The report has no clear introduction and conclusion.	The report's introduction and conclusion do not serve their purpose.	The introduction presents the topic, and the conclusion summarizes it, but they are not complete.	The introduction states the topic and grabs the audience's interest; the conclusion summarizes the main ideas in a satisfying way.
The report is not focused and includes much unnecessary information.	The report includes some unnecessary information.	The report includes one or two unnecessary details.	The report is focused; all of the information is necessary and relevant.
The report includes many mistakes in capitalization.	The report includes some mistakes in capitalization.	The report includes a few mistakes in capitalization.	The report includes no mistakes in capitalization.

Using a Rubric
to Study the Model

Use the rubric to assess Matthew's research report. Remember, you will give 1, 2, 3, or 4 points in each category.

How many points did you give Matthew's report? Discuss each category on the rubric with your classmates. Find words and sentences in the report that support your opinion. Then read Selena's assessment of the report.

Audience

Does the writer explain words that the audience might not understand?

"Yes, he does. First, he explains who the Nez Percé are. I had never heard their name before, so I needed to know that. In the second paragraph, he explains the term **reservation**. I thought that was a good idea. Some people might think that word just means asking for a table in a restaurant!"

Chief Joseph, a Nez Percé, was one of the greatest Native American leaders. There are not many Nez Percé left now. They once lived in the area known today as Idaho, Oregon, and Washington. Peaceful people, they helped explorers who came to their territory in the early 1800s. Later, they accepted the American settlers who lived on their land. Chief Joseph devoted his life to helping and protecting the Nez Percé people.

. . . It tried to force the Nez Percé to move to a reservation in Idaho. A reservation is land that the government set aside for Native Americans. Chief Joseph tried to preserve his people's right to the land where they had lived for hundreds of years. Finally, he did attempt to move his people to the reservation. However, U.S. troops attacked them along the way, and the Nez Percé War began.

Does the writer organize the body of the report so it clearly presents and develops the main points?

> This writer presents his main points in the first sentence of each paragraph. See how he does it in the paragraph below? This way of organizing really made the report easy for me to understand.

Chief Joseph was a brave and intelligent leader. Under his leadership, the Nez Percé fought and won many battles against the U.S. troops. In time, Chief Joseph and other Nez Percé leaders knew they could not win the war. They decided to lead their people into Canada.

Do the introduction and conclusion add to the report by stating the topic and summarizing the main points?

> In his introduction, this writer states the topic and grabs my interest in the first two sentences. Right away, I wondered what had happened to the Nez Percé.

Chief Joseph, a Nez Percé, was one of the greatest Native American leaders. There are not many Nez Percé left now.

> Then in his conclusion, the writer stresses that Chief Joseph was a great American leader. He even quotes the chief. That is a meaningful way to end it, don't you think?

Like many great American leaders, Chief Joseph fought for freedom and equality. When he spoke in Washington, he said, "Treat all men alike. Give them all the same law. Give them all an even chance to live and grow." These are still American ideals today.

Clarification

Does the writer focus the report by including only necessary information?

> Every fact and detail in this report relates to Chief Joseph and the way he helped his people. For example, in the paragraph below, the writer doesn't slow things down by telling us exactly when or how Chief Joseph traveled to Washington. Instead, he stresses what Chief Joseph did when he got there.

Chief Joseph continued to fight for his people. He traveled to Washington, D.C., and spoke to lawmakers there. He told of the suffering of the Nez Percé and convinced the lawmakers to send them back to Idaho. Most of the remaining Nez Percé people still live there today.

Conventions & Skills

Does the writer correctly capitalize proper nouns, proper adjectives, and abbreviations?

> Yes, he does. In the paragraph above, the writer capitalizes all these proper nouns: **Chief Joseph, Washington, D.C., Nez Percé,** and **Idaho.** In other parts of his report, he capitalizes **American,** which is a proper adjective. Throughout the whole report, the writer capitalizes the abbreviation **U.S.** and the first word of every sentence. Good job!

Now it's my turn to write!

I'm going to write my own research report. Follow along, and you will see how I try to use good writing strategies. I will use the model report and the rubric to guide my writing.

SeLeNa

Writer of a Research Report

Name:	Selena
Home:	North Carolina
Hobbies:	playing the piano, writing to my pen pal in Honduras
Favorite Food:	anything with peanut butter in it
Favorite Book:	*Roll of Thunder, Hear My Cry* by Mildred Taylor
Assignment:	research report

Prewriting

Gather
Take notes from the Internet and at least one other source. Cite my sources.

"My family is Mexican American, and many of my relatives have worked on farms. I grew up hearing about Cesar Chavez and all that he did to help farmworkers, especially Mexican Americans. When I found out we were going to write a research report, I decided to write about Cesar Chavez. I was eager to learn more about his life.

"I found a Web site about Cesar Chavez that was created by a person who admired him. However, my teacher asked me not to use it. She said it might have some incorrect information in it. Instead, she helped me find a Web site that was from a library on Latin American culture. I took notes from this Web site and from an interesting book about Cesar Chavez that I found at the library. My teacher reminded me to cite my sources as I took notes."

Citing Sources

When you **cite a source,** you tell readers where you found certain information. The examples below show how to present the information about a source. Pay attention to the order of the information and the use of commas, colons, and periods. Remember that the title of a book should be in italics or underlined. The title of an article should be in quotation marks.

To cite a book:
Author's last name, author's first name. *Book title.* City of publication: publisher, date of publication.

Example: Collins, David R. *Farmworker's Friend: The Story of Cesar Chavez.* Minneapolis: Carolrhoda Books, 1996.

To cite a Web site:
Author (if given), "Title of article." Sponsor of Web site. Date of article. Web site address.

Example: "The Story of Cesar Chavez." Latino Culture: U.S. 25 May 2001. http://latinoculture.about.com.

"Right away, I found interesting information for my report. My teacher had shown us how to put the information on note cards. Each fact or group of closely related facts gets its own note card. Here are three of my note cards. I added headings to my cards, too, so it would be easier to group them by topic later on."

Chavez Family ← heading

Mother - taught him about nonviolence
    and helping others
Father - taught him to stand up for his
    beliefs and for other people ← note

Farmworker's Friend: The Story of
Cesar Chavez, p. 3 ← source

Basic Information on Chavez

Born: March 31, 1927 in Yuma, Arizona
Died: April 23, 1993 in San Luis, Arizona

"Story of Cesar Chavez," p. 2

Chavez's Early Life

Did not like school because he spoke only
Spanish/dropped out in 8th grade to work

"Story of Cesar Chavez," p. 1

Go to page 52 in the **Practice** the Strategy **Notebook!**

Prewriting

Organize
Use my notes to make a support pattern.

" I know from the **Rubric** that organization is important. I had a pile of note cards, and I needed a good way to put them in order. I read through my cards and looked for important points in Cesar Chavez's early life. I could see that his parents had a strong influence on him. I could start there.

"I decided to make a support pattern, which is kind of like an outline. The support pattern helped me organize the information I had found in my research. "

Support Pattern

A **support pattern** is a chart that shows how main points are supported by facts.

Topic: Cesar Chavez

Main Point: Cesar's best teachers were his parents.

Supporting facts
- Mother taught him violence is not a good way to settle problems.
- It is good to help other people.
- Father taught him to stand up for his beliefs.

Expository Writing • Research Report

Main Point: Cesar Chavez never forgot the lessons he learned as a child.

Supporting facts
- Family lost their farm and became migrant workers.
- Mexican Americans were often treated unfairly.
- The life of migrant farmworkers is very hard.

Main Point: As Cesar got older, his beliefs became stronger.

Supporting facts
- He decided he should help migrant farmworkers.
- Farmworkers should have better pay, safer working conditions, and healthier living conditions.
- Nonviolent methods can bring about change.

Main Point: Cesar put his beliefs into action.

Supporting facts
- He registered voters and told Mexican Americans about their rights.
- He formed the National Farm Workers Association, and it became the U.F.W.
- U.F.W. and supporters held boycotts, marched in picket lines, and held strikes without violence.
- Cesar led marches, fasted, worked long hours, and helped improve the lives of the farmworkers.

Go to page 54 in the **Practice** the Strategy **Notebook!**

Drafting

Write
Draft the body of my report. Write a paragraph for each main point on my organizer.

" I've done my research and organized my notes. Now I'm ready to draft the body of my report. I'll write a paragraph for every main point on my support pattern. I'll include supporting facts in each paragraph.

"The **Rubric** reminds me to think about my audience as I write. My classmates will be my audience. I will make sure to explain any words that they might not understand. I want to make it easy for them to learn about Cesar Chavez's life and work.

"You can read part of the body of my report on this page and the next page. Look for the main points. Did I explain any words that are new to you? "

Body

The **body** is the main part of a piece of writing. It comes between the introduction and the conclusion and explains the main ideas.

---

main point

[1st DRAFT]

  Cesar's best teachers were his parents. He was born in Yuma, Arizona, in 1927. He did not like his early school years, partly because Mexican American children were often treated unfairly. Cesar's mother taught him that violence was not the way to settle problems. She encouraged him to help other people. Cesar's father taught him to stand up for his beliefs.

main point ⟶ explain unfamiliar words

Cesar never forgot the lessons he learned as a child. When he was still a boy, his family was swindled, or cheated, out of their farm. They had to become migrant farmworkers in California. A migrant worker moves from place to place to pick crops. There Cesar discovered much more injustice. His family worked in the feilds for long hours and very little pay. They worked from Brawley to Oxnard. They often lived in one-room shacks without running water. His mother's name was Juana, and his father's name was Librado.

main point

As Cesar got older, his beliefs became stronger. He joined the U.S. Navy at age 17. When he was 21, he married a woman named Helen Fabela. All during this time, Cesar believed that the farmworkers should recieve fair pay for their work. He believed that their working conditions should be safer. He knew that their living conditions should be healthier.

Cesar put his beliefs into action. He began by working to register mexican american voters. He told Mexican Americans about their rights in the u.s.a. In 1962, Cesar founded the National Farm Workers association. This union became the united farm workers, or the U.F.W. It used nonviolent ways to bring attention to the farmworkers' problems. u.f.w. members led boycotts, urging people not to buy products from companies that were unfair to migrant workers. Union Members also explain unfamiliar word marched on picket lines and held strikes. Cesar led marches, held press conferences, and fasted (stopped eating). He worked long hours to help the workers get better pay and working conditions.

Go to page 56 in the **Practice the Strategy Notebook!**

Revising

Elaborate

Complete my report by adding an introduction and a conclusion.

> " I included all my main points in the body of my first draft, but I didn't have an introduction or a conclusion. As I read what I had written, I realized that Cesar Chavez was only one man, but he changed many lives. That's what I should stress in my introduction and conclusion! "

Introduction, Conclusion

A good **introduction** immediately grabs the audience's attention and states the topic of the report. The **conclusion** is the last paragraph of a report. It ties up loose ends, summarizes main points, and often restates key ideas from the introduction.

[2nd DRAFT]

introduction

Cesar Chavez was a very determined man. He organized a union with more than 50,000 members, focused attention on migrant workers, and helped change laws. In these ways, he improved the lives of many farmworkers. He was also a self-taught man. He learned many of his most important lessons during his childhood.

conclusion

Cesar Chavez died in 1993, but his dream did not. He inspired many people, and they are continuing his work today. Cesar chavez saw a problem and decided he could do something about it. His life proves that one person can make a huge and lasting difference.

Go to page 57 in the **Practice the Strategy Notebook!**

Revising

Clarify

Delete any unnecessary information.

" Well, by now my research report included all my main points and the supporting facts. When I read my report to my partner, however, she said some parts were TOO detailed. Too many details can confuse readers. I went back and found some unnecessary details. Don't you think these paragraphs will be easier to understand and more interesting if I take out these details? "

READ TO A PARTNER

main point

[3rd DRAFT]

Cesar never forgot the lessons he learned as a child. When he was still a boy, his family was swindled, or cheated, out of their farm. They had to become migrant farmworkers in California. A migrant worker moves from place to place to pick crops. There Cesar discovered much more injustice. His family worked in the fields for long hours and very little pay. They worked from Brawley to Oxnard. They often lived in one-room shacks without running water. His mother's name was Juana, and his father's name was Librado.

unnecessary details

As Cesar got older, his beliefs became stronger. He joined the U.S. Navy at age 17. When he was 21, he married a woman named Helen Fabela. ~~All during this time, Cesar~~ He believed that the farmworkers should receive fair pay for their work. He believed that their working conditions should be safer. He knew that their living conditions should be healthier.

Go to page 58 in the **Practice** the Strategy **Notebook!**

Editing

Proofread

Check to see that I have capitalized words correctly.

> Now I need to proofread my report. I always check my spelling and punctuation. Today, I'll pay special attention to capitalizing the first letter in proper nouns, proper adjectives, initials, and abbreviations. I will draw three lines under each letter that should be a capital. I'll put a slash through any letters that should not be capitals. On the next page, you can see the kinds of corrections I made in part of my report.

Capitalization

- Capitalize the first letter in proper nouns:
  Mexican **A**mericans, **C**alifornia

- Capitalize the first letter in proper adjectives:
  Mexican **A**merican farmworkers, **S**panish language

- Capitalize initials in proper nouns:
  Cesar **E.** Chavez, John **F.** Kennedy

- Capitalize abbreviations of words that are capitalized when written out:
  U.S.A., U.F.W. (United Farm Workers)

Extra Practice
See **Capitalization** (pages CS 10–CS 11) in the back of this book.

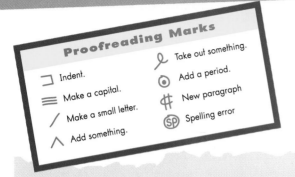

Proofreading Marks

⌐ Indent.

≡ Make a capital.

/ Make a small letter.

∧ Add something.

ℓ Take out something.

⊙ Add a period.

New paragraph

SP Spelling error

[4th DRAFT]

should be capitalized

    Cesar put his beliefs into action. He began by working to register mexican american voters. He told Mexican Americans about their rights in the u.s.a. In 1962, Cesar founded the National Farm Workers association. This union became the united farm workers, or the U.F.W. It used nonviolent ways to bring attention to the farm-workers' problems. u.f.w. members led boycotts, urging people not to buy products from companies that were unfair to migrant work-ers. Union Members also marched on picket lines and held strikes. Cesar led marches, held press conferences, and fasted (stopped eating). He worked long hours to help the workers get better pay and working conditions.

should be capitalized

should not be capitalized

    Cesar Chavez died in 1993, but his dream did not. He inspired many people, and they are continuing his work today. Cesar chavez saw a problem and decided he could do something about it. His life proves that one person can make a huge and lasting difference.

Go to page 59 in the **Practice** the Strategy **Notebook!**

Publishing

Share — Include my written report in my multimedia presentation to the class.

Writer:	Selena
Assignment:	research report
Topic:	Cesar Chavez
Audience:	my classmates
Method of Publication:	include my written report in my multimedia presentation to the class
Reason for Choice:	Many of my classmates have never heard of Cesar Chavez.

"Many of my classmates do not know who Cesar Chavez was. A multimedia presentation will allow them to see and hear him. Our teacher explained that a multimedia presentation can include pictures, charts, and graphs mounted on poster board. It can also include tape recordings or short video clips of speeches. Here's how I put my multimedia presentation together."

1. First, I selected a short video clip of a speech by Cesar Chavez from a Web site.

2. I decided on the order for my presentation. I would play the short video clip, using a computer in our classroom. Then I would read my report.

3. I practiced using the computer to show the video clip. Then I practiced reading my report until I could do it easily.

Cesar Chavez

by Selena

Cesar Chavez was a very determined man. He organized a union with more than 50,000 members, focused attention on migrant workers, and helped change laws. In these ways, he improved the lives of many farmworkers. He was also a self-taught man. He learned many of his most important lessons during his childhood.

Cesar's best teachers were his parents. He was born in Yuma, Arizona, in 1927. He did not like his early school years, partly because Mexican American children were often treated unfairly. Cesar's mother taught him that violence was not the way to settle problems. She encouraged him to help other people. Cesar's father taught him to stand up for his beliefs.

Cesar never forgot the lessons he learned as a child. When he was still a boy, his family was swindled, or cheated, out of their farm. They had to become migrant farmworkers in California. A migrant worker moves from place to place to pick crops. There Cesar discovered much more injustice. His family worked in the fields for long hours and very little pay. They often lived in one-room shacks without running water.

As Cesar got older, his beliefs became stronger. He believed that the farmworkers should receive fair pay for their work. He believed that their working conditions should be safer. He knew that their living conditions should be healthier.

Cesar put his beliefs into action. He began by working to register Mexican American voters. He told Mexican Americans about their rights in the U.S.A. In 1962, Cesar founded the

National Farm Workers Association. This union became the United Farm Workers, or the U.F.W. It used nonviolent ways to bring attention to the farmworkers' problems. U.F.W. members led boycotts, urging people not to buy products from companies that were unfair to migrant workers. Union members also marched on picket lines and held strikes. Cesar led marches, held press conferences, and fasted (stopped eating). He worked long hours to help the workers get better pay and working conditions.

Cesar Chavez died in 1993, but his dream did not. He inspired many people, and they are continuing his work today. Cesar Chavez saw a problem and decided he could do something about it. His life proves that one person can make a huge and lasting difference.

Sources

Collins, David R. Farmworker's Friend: The Story of Cesar Chavez. Minneapolis: Carolrhoda Books, 1996.

"The Story of Cesar Chavez." Latino Culture: U.S. 25 May 2001. http://latinoculture.about.com.

USING the Rubric for Assessment

Go to pages 60–61 in the **Practice** the Strategy **Notebook!** Use that rubric to assess Selena's paper. Try using the rubric to assess your own writing.

EXPOSITORY writing

Compare-and-Contrast Essay

In this chapter, you will practice one kind of expository writing: a **compare-and-contrast essay**.

A **compare-and-contrast essay** tells how two or more things are the same (compare) or different (contrast).

On the next page is a compare-and-contrast essay. Read these questions. Then read the essay, keeping the questions in mind.

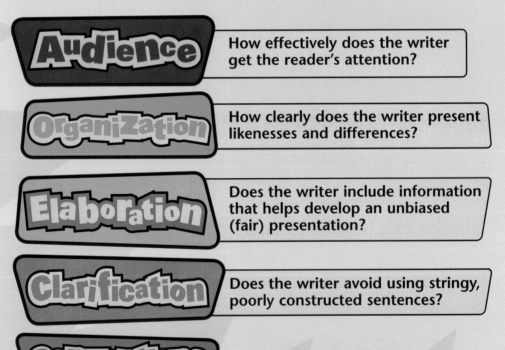

Audience — How effectively does the writer get the reader's attention?

Organization — How clearly does the writer present likenesses and differences?

Elaboration — Does the writer include information that helps develop an unbiased (fair) presentation?

Clarification — Does the writer avoid using stringy, poorly constructed sentences?

Conventions & Skills — Does the writer capitalize and punctuate titles correctly?

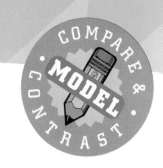

Television Goes to the Movies

by Karen Parkhill

"Danger, Will Robinson! Danger!" Do you recognize that line? It's from the movie Lost in Space—and from a TV show!

Some television shows are turned into movies. Sometimes the TV show and the movie are a lot alike, but sometimes they're very different.

One good example is Lost in Space. The 1998 movie was based on the 1960s TV show. The film and the TV show have much in common. The main similarity is the storyline: the Robinson family is lost in space. The main characters are also the same. John and Maureen Robinson head the Robinson family. Their children are named Judy, Penny, and Will. Will has a talking robot as his sidekick. The cast includes the pilot, Major Don West, and the evil Dr. Smith. The good guys on TV are still the good guys in the movie. The bad guys are still the bad guys.

How are the film and the TV show different? First of all, movies are longer, usually about two hours. A TV episode lasts only 30 to 60 minutes, but a series can go on for years. The movie Lost in Space is less than two hours long. The television series Lost in Space lasted three years.

The biggest difference between the show and the movie is in the special effects. Computer-made special effects did not exist in 1964. For the TV show, tiny model spaceships were built to make the sets seem bigger. Ocean waves were created in a huge water tank. Actors in costumes played aliens and monsters. Today, if you watch a TV episode of Lost in Space, you might laugh at the effects. Still, you have to admit that they were very creative. For the movie Lost in Space, computer experts created special graphics, animation, and sound effects. The two-hour television pilot cost around $600,000 to make. The two-hour movie cost almost $90,000,000.

Lost in Space is just one of many TV shows that have been made into movies. This movie and TV show are much alike, but they're different enough to make each one interesting in its own way.

Using a Rubric

A rubric is a tool that lists "what counts" for a piece of writing. You assign 1, 2, 3, or 4 points in certain categories to show how well the author handled those skills. The questions on page 122 were used to make this rubric.

"Hi! I'm Henry. I'm learning to write a compare-and-contrast essay, too. What did you think of the essay you just read? To evaluate it, read the questions in this rubric. Then read the information for each question. We'll be using this rubric to rate the essay."

Audience

How effectively does the writer get the reader's attention?

Organization

How clearly does the writer present likenesses and differences?

Elaboration

Does the writer include information that helps develop an unbiased (fair) presentation?

Clarification

Does the writer avoid using stringy, poorly constructed sentences?

Conventions & Skills

Does the writer capitalize and punctuate titles correctly?

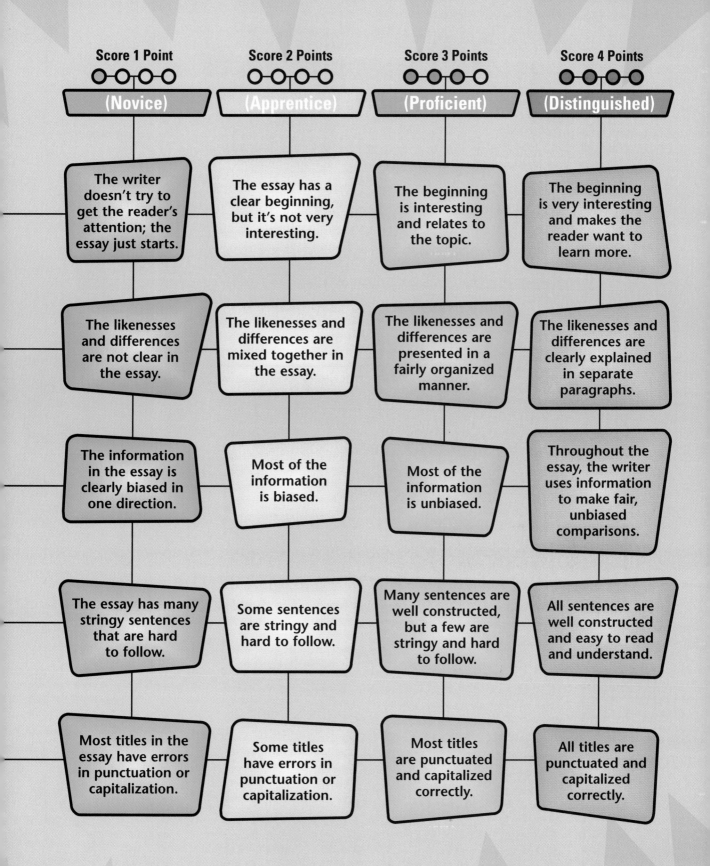

Score 1 Point

(Novice)

The writer doesn't try to get the reader's attention; the essay just starts.

The likenesses and differences are not clear in the essay.

The information in the essay is clearly biased in one direction.

The essay has many stringy sentences that are hard to follow.

Most titles in the essay have errors in punctuation or capitalization.

Score 2 Points

(Apprentice)

The essay has a clear beginning, but it's not very interesting.

The likenesses and differences are mixed together in the essay.

Most of the information is biased.

Some sentences are stringy and hard to follow.

Some titles have errors in punctuation or capitalization.

Score 3 Points

(Proficient)

The beginning is interesting and relates to the topic.

The likenesses and differences are presented in a fairly organized manner.

Most of the information is unbiased.

Many sentences are well constructed, but a few are stringy and hard to follow.

Most titles are punctuated and capitalized correctly.

Score 4 Points

(Distinguished)

The beginning is very interesting and makes the reader want to learn more.

The likenesses and differences are clearly explained in separate paragraphs.

Throughout the essay, the writer uses information to make fair, unbiased comparisons.

All sentences are well constructed and easy to read and understand.

All titles are punctuated and capitalized correctly.

Using a Rubric

to Study the Model

With your classmates, discuss each question on the rubric. Look for sentences and paragraphs in the model that help you answer each question. Then use the rubric to evaluate Karen Parkhill's essay.

Audience

How effectively does the writer get the reader's attention?

"" The writer uses a familiar quotation and a question to get my attention. I was interested right away. I wanted to learn more about the two versions of Lost in Space. ""

"Danger, Will Robinson! Danger!" Do you recognize that line? It's from the movie Lost in Space—and from a TV show!

How clearly does the writer present likenesses and differences?

" I like the way the writer puts the likenesses and differences in separate paragraphs. That makes it easier to understand how the movie and TV show are the same and different, don't you think? "

The film and the TV show have much in common. The main similarity is the storyline: the Robinson family is lost in space. The main characters are also the same. . . .

The biggest difference between the show and the movie is in the special effects. Computer-made special effects did not exist in 1964. . . .

Does the writer include information that helps develop an unbiased (fair) presentation?

" Our teacher told us that compare-and-contrast essays are not meant to be persuasive. This writer knows that. She provides information but keeps her opinions to herself. She doesn't try to convince me that the movie or the TV show is better. This writer keeps her presentation fair. "

Lost in Space is just one of many TV shows that have been made into movies. The movie and TV show are much alike, but they're different enough to make each one interesting in its own way.

"I didn't see any stringy sentences in this essay. The writer keeps most of her sentences rather short and to the point. Even her longer sentences are easy to read and understand. They are well organized and have only one main idea."

The main characters are also the same. John and Maureen Robinson head the Robinson family. Their children are named Judy, Penny, and Will. Will has a talking robot as his sidekick. The cast includes the pilot, Major Don West, and the evil Dr. Smith. The good guys on TV are still the good guys in the movie. The bad guys are still the bad guys.

"The writer remembered to underline Lost in Space and capitalize the important words in it. She even knew that the titles of movies and television series are treated the same way."

The movie Lost in Space is less than two hours long. The television series Lost in Space lasted three years.

Now it's my turn to write!

I'm going to write my own compare-and-contrast essay. Follow along to see how I do my best to use good writing strategies. I'm going to use the model and the rubric to help me.

HeNRy

Writer of a
Compare-and-Contrast Essay

Name:	Henry
Home:	Massachusetts
Hobbies:	baseball, learning about American history
Favorite Teacher:	Ms. Lillard, history teacher
Favorite Book:	*Baseball's Greatest Games* by Dan Gutman
Assignment:	compare-and-contrast essay

Prewriting

Gather — Interview others and take notes.

> I love baseball. I love to watch it, play it, talk about it, and read about it. Lucky for me, we have a professional baseball team right here in Boston.
>
> "When my teacher asked us to write a compare-and-contrast essay, I thought about the Red Sox game I went to last month. I knew my friend Eli had watched the same game on television. I thought about how seeing it at the stadium was different from seeing it on TV. I decided to interview Eli and get his thoughts about it. Here are some of the questions I asked him and the notes I took on his answers.

Interview

An **interview** is a way to gather information. In an interview, you ask someone prepared questions and record his or her thoughts or opinions.

Questions for Eli

Q: What's the best thing about watching a ball game on TV?

    announcers give history, tell stories

    stats are always on screen

    close-up shots and instant replays

    always have a good view

Q: Have you been to a game at the ballpark?

    Yes

Q: Is there anything you miss about the stadium when you watch at home?

    yes, the crowd

    fun to be with other fans

    smell of popcorn, peanuts, and hot dogs

Go to page 62 in the **Practice the Strategy Notebook!**

Expository Writing · Compare-and-Contrast Essay

PreWriting

Organize

Organize my interview notes into an attribute chart. Include my own ideas, too.

"I know from the **Rubric** that organization is important. I looked at my notes from my interview with Eli and thought about my own experiences at the park. I needed a way to organize my notes and ideas. I decided to make a chart."

Attribute Chart

An attribute is a quality of something. An **attribute chart** can help organize information about how two things are alike and different.

Game on TV	Attribute	Game at the Stadium
walk to couch	Getting There	take a car or bus, find a parking space
close-ups, instant replays, stats on screen	What You See	whole field, stats on scoreboard
announcers giving history, stories; crowd cheering in the distance	What You Hear	crowd cheering all around you; announcer naming players and so on
no crowds, no waiting in lines, no interruptions	Surroundings	lots of people, have to wait in lines, fun to share experience
always comfortable	How You Feel	could be hot, cold, soaked in a rainstorm

Go to page 64 in the **Practice** the Strategy **Notebook!**

Drafting

Write
Draft my essay. Discuss the likenesses and differences in separate paragraphs.

" Now I'm ready to write. I know from the **Rubric** that I need to explain likenesses and differences in separate paragraphs. As I start my draft, I'll concentrate on getting my ideas down on paper and on keeping the likenesses and differences separate. I'll do my best with spelling and grammar. I can correct any mistakes I make later.

"On this page and the next one, you can read my first draft. Do you see how I put the likenesses and the differences in separate paragraphs? "

[1st DRAFT]

Live or Televised?

Baseball is America's favorite pastime. Its also mine. I love books like Baseball's greatest Games by Dan Gutman. My favorite television show is Baseball Today. I even know a poem about baseball, Casey at the Bat. The Boston Red Sox is my favorite team. I watch all the Red Sox games, sometimes on television and sometimes at the stadium.

likenesses

Is watching a game on television the same as watching it from the stands? Either way, you're going to see lots of action. You're also going to get lots of information about the players. At the ballpark, you can look at the scoreboard and see who is at bat and his jersey number. You can also get the count of balls, strikes, and outs. The scoreboard on a television screen is similar. It shows the score and the batting count right on your screen.

Expository Writing • Compare-and-Contrast Essay

There's always an announcer at the ballpark. The announcer repeats information from the scoreboard and tells who is stepping up to the plate, who is pitching, and so on. Television announcers talk a lot, too. They give stats and news about teams and players. They also tell stories about famous players of the past.

statistics

Even though you can catch all the action from your couch or from the stands, there are big differences. Television lets you watch the game from home. You don't have to catch a bus or ride in a car to the game and you don't have to find a parking space and you don't have to buy a ticket. If you're watching a game on television, you can see instant replays. Most ballparks can't show replays. At the ballpark, you can see the whole field at once but, on television, cameras follow the ball and take lots of close-up shots of players.

Another thing that's different is the crowd. When you watch a game on television, you might be watching alone. When you're in the stands, you're with hundreds of other fans who share your excite-ment. There's nothing like watching a game in person!

You know, it really doesn't matter where or how you watch baseball. From the stands or from your couch, it's fun!

Go to page 65 in the **Practice** the Strategy **Notebook!**

Revising

Elaborate
Make sure the information I add helps to develop an unbiased presentation.

"After I finished my first draft, I read it over. I realized that I must still be a little excited about the last game I saw at the stadium. In one paragraph, it seemed like I was trying to convince everyone to go to a game. I didn't always give television watching a fair shake. I knew I had to make some changes so the comparisons were fair. My first draft was too biased toward going to the stadium."

READ TO MYSELF

Bias

A **bias** is a preference. Someone who is biased prefers one thing over another. Biased writing does not present both sides of an issue fairly and equally.

[2nd DRAFT]

added benefits of watching at home to make essay fair —
> No one will interrupt you to pass a bag of peanuts. If you have to go to the bathroom, you won't have to stand in line and miss a great play.

Another thing that's different is the crowd. When you watch a game on television, you might be watching alone. When you're in the stands, you're with hundreds of other fans who share your excite- Sometimes that makes it more fun. ment. ~~There's nothing like watching a game in person!~~

replaced biased statement with a more neutral one

Go to page 67 in the **Practice** the Strategy **Notebook!**

Revising

Clarify
Rewrite stringy sentences to make them clearer.

> When I read my essay again, I noticed that some of my sentences were stringy and confusing. I saw where I could divide some of them into two sentences to make them clearer. One of my sentences was so long that I made it into three sentences!

Stringy Sentences

Stringy sentences are so long that readers forget the beginning of the sentence by the time they reach the end. Stringy sentences should be divided into two or more shorter sentences.

[3rd DRAFT]

Even though you can catch all the action from your couch or from the stands, there are big differences. Television lets you watch the

revised stringy sentence — game from home. You don't have to catch a bus or ride in a car to the game, and you don't have to find a parking space, and you don't even have to buy a ticket. If you're watching a game on television, you can see instant replays. Most ballparks can't show replays. At the ballpark, you can see the whole field at once. However, but, on television, **revised stringy sentence** cameras follow the ball and take close-up shots of players.

Go to page 68 in the **Practice the Strategy Notebook!**

Editing

Proofread

Check to see that all titles are capitalized and punctuated correctly.

> Now I need to look for errors in my essay. I always check for capitalization and spelling mistakes. I know from the **Rubric** that I need to check the titles in my essay. I have to make sure I've used the correct punctuation and that I've underlined certain titles.

Titles

Capitalize the first word, last word, and all other words except articles, short prepositions, and conjunctions.

Example: Jim Prime and Bill Nowlan wrote <u>Tales From the Red Sox Dugout.</u>

Underline or italicize the titles of books, movies, and television series.

Example: <u>The Red Sox Reader</u> is a book by Dan Riley.

Use quotation marks around titles of songs, stories, poems, and television episodes.

Example: America's favorite baseball song, "Take Me Out to the Ball Game," was written in 1909.

Extra Practice

See **Titles** (pages CS 12–CS 13) in the back of this book.

[4th DRAFT]

Capitalize and underline book title.

Live or Televised?

Baseball is America's favorite pastime. It's also mine. I love books like Baseball's greatest Games by Dan Gutman. My favorite television show is Baseball Today. I even know a poem about baseball, Casey at the Bat. The Boston Red Sox is my favorite team. I watch all the Red Sox games, sometimes on television and sometimes at the stadium.

Capitalize and underline TV series title.

Put quotation marks around poem title.

Go to page 69 in the **Practice** the Strategy **Notebook!**

Publishing

Share Put my essay in a time capsule.

Writer: Henry
Assignment: compare-and-contrast essay
Topic: televised versus live baseball games
Audience: classmates
Method of Publication: time capsule
Reason for Choice: My essay will help show what everyday life is like right now.

"The students in my class are each making their own time capsule. We're going to open them in 25 years and see how things have changed during that time. I thought my essay about live and televised baseball games would remind me of how we had fun these days. Here's what I did to get my essay ready for my time capsule."

1. First, I checked my essay one more time to make sure it was as good as I could make it.

2. Then I found some baseball pictures in a clip-art program and added them to my pages.

3. I put the essay in an envelope and wrote the title of the essay and the date on the envelope.

4. Last, I added the envelope to my time capsule.

Live or Televised?
by Henry

Baseball is America's favorite pastime. It's also mine. I love books like Baseball's Greatest Games by Dan Gutman. My favorite television show is Baseball Today. I even know a poem about baseball, "Casey at the Bat." The Boston Red Sox is my favorite team. I watch all the Red Sox games, sometimes on television and sometimes at the stadium.

Is watching a game on television the same as watching it from the stands? Either way, you're going to see lots of action. You're also going to get a lot of information about the players. At the ballpark, you can look at the scoreboard and see who is at bat. You can also get the count of balls, strikes, and outs. A television scoreboard is similar. It shows the score and the batting count right on your screen.

There's always an announcer at the ballpark. The announcer repeats information from the scoreboard and identifies the players. Television announcers talk a lot, too. They give statistics and news about teams and players. They also tell stories about famous players of the past.

Even though you can catch all the action from your couch or from the stands, there are big differences. Television lets you watch the game from home. You don't have to catch a bus or ride in a car to the game. You don't have to find a parking space. You don't even have to buy a ticket. If you're watching a game on television, you can see instant replays. Most ballparks can't show replays. At the ballpark, you can see the whole field at once. However, television cameras follow the ball and take close-up shots of players.

Another thing that's different is the crowd. When you watch a game on television, you might be watching alone. No one will interrupt you to pass a bag of peanuts. If you have to go to the bathroom, you won't have to stand in line and miss a great play. When you're in the stands, you're with hundreds of other fans who share your excitement. Sometimes that makes it more fun.

You know, it really doesn't matter where or how you watch baseball. From the stands or from your couch, it's great entertainment!

USING the Rubric for Assessment

Go to pages 70–71 in the **Practice** the Strategy **Notebook!** Use that rubric to assess Henry's paper. Try using the rubric to assess your own writing.

your own EXPOSITORY writing

Social Studies

Put the strategies you practiced in this unit to work to write your own compare-and-contrast essay, research report, or both! You can:

- develop the writing you did in the Your Own Writing pages of the *Practice the Strategy Notebook*;

- pick an idea below and write something new;

- choose another idea of your own.

Be sure to follow the steps in the writing process. Use the rubrics in this unit to assess your writing.

Research Report

- how immigrants enter the United States
- how the Secret Service protects the president of the United States
- how volunteering affects our community
- how a certain service organization helps people during disasters

Compare-and-Contrast Essay

- the climate in two states
- the Declaration of Independence and the Constitution
- lifestyles in the United States and another country
- the South Pole and the North Pole

portfolio

School–Home Connection

Keep a writing portfolio. Think about adding the activities from the *Practice the Strategy Notebook* to your writing portfolio. You may want to take your portfolio home to share.

NARRATIVE

writing

tells the reader a story.

1
Fable

2
Mystery

NARRATIVE writing

Fable

In this chapter, you will practice another kind of narrative writing: a **fable**.

In a **fable,** the writer often uses talking animals or objects as the main characters. These main characters teach a lesson, which is called a **moral**.

The story on the next page is a fable. Study the following questions. Then read the fable, keeping the questions in mind.

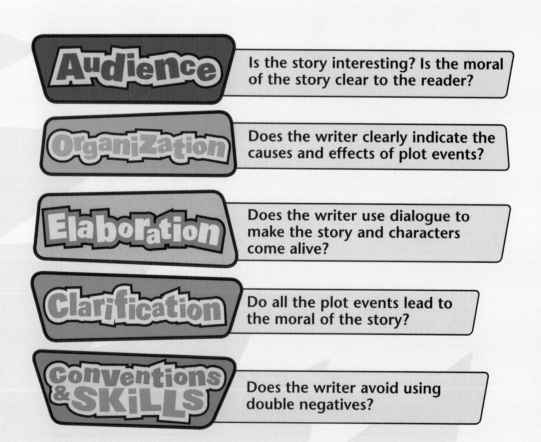

Audience — Is the story interesting? Is the moral of the story clear to the reader?

Organization — Does the writer clearly indicate the causes and effects of plot events?

Elaboration — Does the writer use dialogue to make the story and characters come alive?

Clarification — Do all the plot events lead to the moral of the story?

Conventions & Skills — Does the writer avoid using double negatives?

THE FOX AND THE CROW

retold by Rachel Randall

One bitterly cold winter day, a skinny fox was walking through the woods. His red fur was scraggly, and his tongue was hanging out of his mouth. The fox was in a terrible mood because he hadn't had anything to eat for days. "Man, I'm hungry," he said to himself. "If I don't find something to eat soon, I'm toast!"

Just then, a crow flew overhead and landed on a tree branch near the fox. In the crow's beak was an enormous piece of cheese. The fox's mouth watered as he gazed admiringly at the crow's cheese. Its delicious smell almost drove him crazy. *I've got to get my paws on that cheese,* thought the fox.

Then a smile crept across the fox's lean and hungry face, and he sauntered slowly over to the tree. Looking up at the crow, the fox said in a friendly voice, "Hey, Crow! How's it going?"

The crow glanced down at the fox with suspicion.

"I was just thinking about how sharp you look with those sleek feathers," the fox said smoothly. "Black is really your color, and I love the color of your eyes, too."

The crow began to smile.

"I bet you're a terrific singer," continued the fox. "Any bird that looks as cool as you do has to have a great voice. I wonder if maybe you could just sing one song for me?"

The crow was so pleased at the fox's compliments that she opened her beak and let out her loudest caw. However, the moment she opened her mouth, the cheese fell to the ground with a plop. The fox strolled over to the huge piece of cheese and quickly snapped it up.

"Thanks a million, Crow," he said, smacking his lips. "Because you were so generous to give me your cheese, I'm going to give you a little piece of advice for the future—*Don't trust people who flatter you.*"

Using a Rubric

A rubric is a good way to assess a piece of writing. It can also help you improve your own writing. Rubrics are easy to use. You simply assign 1, 2, 3, or 4 points in each category in the rubric.

Remember the questions you studied on page 142? Those questions were used to make the rubric you see here.

 Hi! My name is Brian. I'm learning how to write a fable, too. What did you think of the fable on page 143? Let's use this rubric to see how well the fable was written. Review the questions in each category in the rubric. Next, read the scoring information for each category. Then, on pages 146–148, you and I will use this rubric to evaluate the fable. **"**

Is the story interesting? Is the moral of the story clear to the reader?

Does the writer clearly indicate the causes and effects of plot events?

Does the writer use dialogue to make the story and characters come alive?

Do all the plot events lead to the moral of the story?

Does the writer avoid using double negatives?

Score 1 Point	Score 2 Points	Score 3 Points	Score 4 Points
(Novice)	**(Apprentice)**	**(Proficient)**	**(Distinguished)**
The story is not very interesting and does not seem to have a moral.	The story is somewhat interesting. A moral is suggested but not clearly indicated.	The story holds the reader's attention. The moral is somewhat clear.	The story is very interesting, and the moral is very clear.
The causes and effects of plot events are not clear.	Some causes and effects are clear, but most are not.	Most causes and effects are clear.	All causes and effects are clear and well connected.
There is little or no dialogue.	There is some dialogue, but it is not interesting.	The dialogue is mostly interesting.	The dialogue is very interesting and makes the story and characters come alive.
Many of the plot events are not related to the moral of the story.	Several plot events are not related to the moral.	A few plot events are not related to the moral.	All of the plot events lead to the moral of the story.
The story contains many double negatives.	The story contains several double negatives.	The story contains a few double negatives.	The story contains no double negatives.

Using a Rubric

to Study the Model

Use the rubric to evaluate the fable about the fox and the crow. Remember, you will give 1, 2, 3, or 4 points in each category.

How many points did you give the fable? Discuss each category on the rubric with your classmates. Find words and sentences in the fable that support your decisions. Then read Brian's assessment of the fable.

Is the story interesting? Is the moral of the story clear to the reader?

" Absolutely! When I started reading this story, I read straight through to the end. As for the moral, I knew right away that the crow was being foolish to listen to the fox's compliments. At the end of the fable, the fox gave her some advice. Remember that part? That's where the writer made the moral of the story really clear. "

"Thanks a million, Crow," he said, smacking his lips. "Because you were so generous to give me your cheese, I'm going to give you a little piece of advice for the future—*Don't trust people who flatter you.*"

Does the writer clearly indicate the causes and effects of plot events?

> Definitely! For example, in the first paragraph, the writer explains the cause of the fox's bad mood: the poor guy is starving! I got the feeling then that he was going to come up with some kind of plan to find something to eat.

One bitterly cold winter day, a skinny fox was walking through the woods. His red fur was scraggly, and his tongue was hanging out of his mouth. The fox was in a terrible mood because he hadn't had anything to eat for days. "Man, I'm hungry," he said to himself. "If I don't find something to eat soon, I'm toast!"

Does the writer use dialogue to make the story and characters come alive?

> The dialogue in this fable makes the characters seem real. The writer lets me learn about the fox's personality by the words he uses. I can tell how sly the fox is by the way he piles on the compliments.

Looking up at the crow, the fox said in a friendly voice, "Hey, Crow! How's it going?"

The crow glanced down at the fox with suspicion.

"I was just thinking about how sharp you look with those sleek feathers," the fox said smoothly. "Black is really your color, and I love the color of your eyes, too."

Clarification

Do all the plot events lead to the moral of the story?

> Everything that happened in the story led to the moral. Look how the clever fox compliments the crow's feathers and her eyes. It's all part of his trick to get her to open her mouth and drop the cheese.

"I bet you're a terrific singer," continued the fox. "Any bird that looks as cool as you do has to have a great voice. I wonder if maybe you could just sing one song for me?"

Conventions & Skills

Does the writer avoid using double negatives?

> This fable has absolutely no double negatives. The fox 'hadn't had anything to eat for days.' He says, 'If I don't find something to eat soon, I'm toast!' See? No double negatives!

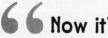 **Now it's my turn to write!**

I'm going to write my own fable. Follow along, and you will see how I do my best to use the rubric to practice good writing strategies. I will also use the model fable to guide my writing.

BriaN

Writer of a Fable

Name: Brian
Home: New Mexico
Hobbies: chess, raising sheep, collecting political campaign buttons
Favorite Sport: track and field
Favorite Book: *Jim Ugly* by Sid Fleischman
Assignment: fable

Prewriting

Gather

Pick a fable that interests me. Take notes on it so I can rewrite it in my own words.

❝ I help raise the sheep and lambs on our family's ranch in New Mexico. When I looked through a book of fables, the one that caught my eye was **The Boy Who Cried Wolf**. I've never actually had to protect my lambs from a wolf, but I do have to chase away the neighbors' dogs sometimes! ❞

Fable, Moral

A **fable** is a short story that often uses talking animals or objects as the main characters. It teaches a moral. A **moral** is a lesson taught through a fable. For example, the moral of *The Fox and the Crow* is "Don't trust flatterers."

❝ When our teacher asked us to rewrite a fable, I started thinking about how I could rewrite **The Boy Who Cried Wolf** with a kid like me as the main character. The original fable was set in ancient times, but mine could take place now, in New Mexico. Here are some notes I took about the plot of the fable. ❞

The Boy Who Cried Wolf

- A boy got bored watching the sheep.
- He decided it would be funny to cry wolf and trick the villagers into running out to the pasture.
- His trick worked several times—all the people came running and the boy laughed.
- Then a real wolf came.
- When the boy cried wolf this time, nobody came.
- Moral: nobody will believe someone who lies all the time, even when he's telling the truth.

Go to page 72 in the **Practice** the Strategy **Notebook!**

Prewriting

Organize
Organize the plot events using a cause-and-effect chain.

❝ I know from the **Rubric** that organization is important. I decided to use my notes about the fable to make a cause-and-effect chain that will show how one thing leads to another. You can see the first part of my chain on this page. When I finish my chain, I'll have the whole plot in it. This will help me make sure my own fable is well organized. ❞

Cause-and-Effect Chain

A **cause-and-effect chain** shows the reasons (causes) for certain events or results (effects). In this chain, an effect can lead to a new cause.

Cause
Boy got bored watching the flock.

Effect
Boy decided to cry, "Wolf!"

Cause
Villagers came running.

Effect
Boy laughed at them.

Cause
Villagers stopped believing him.

Effect
They did not come the next time he called.

Go to page 74 in the **Practice Notebook!** the Strategy

Drafting

Write

Draft my retelling of the fable. Make sure the causes and effects are clear.

"Now I'm ready to write. I'll use my cause-and-effect chain to make sure I include all the events in the original fable. I'll change some of the details, so it will be the same story, told in a different way.

"I also need to keep in mind my audience—my classmates. To make the fable more interesting to them, I'll use language that kids use every day.

"As I write my draft, I'll concentrate on getting the main parts of the fable down on paper. I will work on making clear connections between causes and effects.

I'll do my best with spelling and grammar now, too. I'll check for any mistakes when I edit.

"You can read the first part of my draft on the next page. Do you think it's interesting so far?"

The Boy Who Cried Wolf

A boy named Michael looked after a flock of sheep for a rancher in his town. The rancher lived in the high plains of northern new Mexico. The rancher, Mr. Baker, had given Michael a cell phone. ~~The cell phone cost~~ The boy was to use the cell phone to call him in case wolves, dogs, or coyotes attacked the flock of sheep.

Michael got bored just sitting under a tree watching the sheep all day long. Stupid sheep, he thought to himself, all they do is walk around and munch grass. ~~I think grass tastes terrible.~~ One day   **cause**
especially
when he was bored with his job, Michael had an idea. He pulled the cell phone out of his pocket and dialed Mr. Baker's number. When the rancher answered, Michael told him a pack of coyotes was attacking the sheep. ← **effect**

cause
Within ten minutes, the boy saw the rancher's truck speeding across the plain, a large tail of dust trailing after it. Mr. Baker stopped the truck at the top of the pasture and jumped out. All he saw was the sheep munching peacefully on the green grass near the stream.
effect
Michael was laughing wildly. He thought Mr. Baker looked funny when he jumped out of the truck.

Mr. Baker was not amused ~~and he looked really angry.~~ He spoke in an angry voice, telling Michael that it was wrong to play a trick on him.

the Strategy
Go to page 75 in the **Practice ⋀ Notebook!**

Revising

Elaborate

Add dialogue to make the story and characters come alive.

" After I finished my first draft, I decided that it was okay, but not as exciting as I had hoped. Then I remembered what the **Rubric** said about dialogue. That's what my fable needed! Some dialogue would give my story pizzazz!

"Dialogue could also help me let readers know what my characters are really like. "

Dialogue

Dialogue is the talking between characters in a story.

[2nd DRAFT]

Michael got bored just sitting under a tree watching the sheep all day long. Stupid sheep, he thought to himself, all they do is walk around and munch grass. One day when he was especially bored with his job, Michael had an idea. He pulled the cell phone out of his pocket and dialed Mr. ~added dialogue~ Baker's number. When the rancher answered, Michael screamed into the phone, "Mr. Baker! Mr. Baker! A pack of coyotes is attacking the sheep! Hurry, it's awful!"

Go to page 77 in the Practice the Strategy Notebook!

Revising

Clarify
Make sure that all the plot events lead to the moral of the fable.

66 After I read more of my fable to myself, I noticed another thing. One part, when Michael takes a walk because he's bored, didn't help teach the moral of the story. Then I remembered that the **Rubric** says all the plot events should lead to the moral.

    "I think my fable will be more interesting after I take that part out. Taking away something that doesn't belong will make the whole story better! What do you think? **99**

(READ TO MYSELF)

[3rd DRAFT]

    After a few more days, however, Michael grew even more bored than before. He decided to take a walk up a hillside to find out how far he could see. After a long walk, he finally reached the top of the hill. He gasped when he realized he could see for 30 miles or more! ⟵ *not needed*

    He looked at the cell phone lying on the ground next to him. He thought about how funny Mr. Baker looked when he found out Michael had played a trick on him. Then Michael picked up the cell phone and played the same trick again.

Go to page 78 in the **Practice** the Strategy **Notebook!**

Narrative Writing • Fable   **155**

Proofread

Check to see that I have not used double negatives.

> My fable is pretty much finished now, but I still have to proofread it. I'll check my spelling, capitalization, and punctuation, like I always do. I also need to make sure that I haven't used any double negatives. You can read part of my story and see some of the mistakes I fixed on the next page.

Double Negatives

Use only one **negative** in a sentence. Negatives include words such as *no, not, nothing, none, never, nobody,* and *no one.* A sentence should not contain more than one negative. This error is called a **double negative**.

Incorrect: The man **didn't** say **nothing** when he heard the news.

Correct: The man said **nothing** when he heard the news.
The man **didn't** say anything when he heard the news.

Incorrect: Cody did **not** see **nobody** because it was so dark.

Correct: Cody saw **nobody** because it was so dark.
Cody did **not** see anybody because it was so dark.

Extra Practice
See **Double Negatives** (pages CS 14–CS 15) in the back of this book.

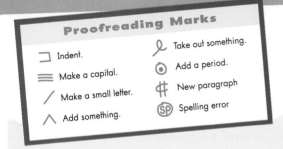

[4th DRAFT]

This time, Mr. Baker was even angrier. He told Michael that if he ever played that trick again, he would lose his job. Michael promised he wouldn't ~~never~~ ∧trick Mr. Baker again.

A week later, michael was sitting under a tree watching the sheep. Out of the corner of his eye, he saw something creeping toward a sheep on the edge of the flock⊙ He

anything

hadn't ever seen ~~nothing~~∧like it before!

corrected double negative

Michael shaded his eyes against the bright sun and saw that the creeping animal was a coyote. Then he saw three

attacked

more. As he watched in horror, the coyotes ~~attacking~~∧the poor sheep. The sheep went down with a terrible bleating cry. The rest of the ~~the~~ sheep started to run.

SP r

With ∧tembling fingers, Michael dialed Mr. Baker's number on the cell phone. When the rancher answered, Michael

are

cried, "Mr. Baker! Come quick! Coyotes ~~is~~∧attacking the sheep!"

the Strategy

Go to page 79 in the **Practice** ∧ **Notebook!**

Publishing

Share
Illustrate my fable and make it into a book for the classroom library.

Writer:	Brian
Assignment:	fable
Topic:	*The Boy Who Cried Wolf*
Audience:	classmates
Method of Publication:	make an illustrated book
Reason for Choice:	to add to the classroom library

"Our class has a library where kids can add things they especially like or have written themselves. That way, other students can read the books, stories, and essays that we all write. Here's what I did to get my fable ready to place in the classroom library."

1. First, I reviewed my fable and listed scenes that would make good illustrations. Then I chose three of them.

2. I used my computer to make a neat copy of the fable, leaving space for three illustrations.

3. Then I drew the illustrations on the pages I had chosen. (For my last story assignment, I used clip art from a Web site.)

4. I placed my finished fable in the library.

The Boy Who Cried Wolf

retold and illustrated by Brian

A boy named Michael looked after a flock of sheep for a rancher in his town. The rancher lived in the high plains of northern New Mexico. The rancher, Mr. Baker, had given Michael a cell phone. The boy was to use the cell phone to call him in case wolves, dogs, or coyotes attacked the flock of sheep.

Michael got bored just sitting under a tree watching the sheep all day long. Stupid sheep, he thought to himself, all they do is walk around and munch grass. One day, when he was especially bored with his job, Michael had an idea. He pulled the cell phone out of his pocket and dialed Mr. Baker's number.

When the rancher answered, Michael cried, "Mr. Baker! Come Quick! Coyotes are attacking the sheep! Hurry, it's awful!"

Within ten minutes, the boy saw the rancher's truck speeding across the plain, a large tail of dust trailing after it. Mr. Baker stopped the truck at the top of the pasture and jumped out. All he saw was the sheep munching peacefully on the green grass near the stream.

Michael was laughing wildly. "You should have seen the look on your face when you jumped out of the truck."

Mr. Baker was not amused. "Do you realize that I drove up here as fast as I could?" he asked in an angry voice. "And what do I find when I get here? You laughing and the sheep safe and sound!"

"OK," said Michael between giggles. "I'm sorry I made you come all the way up here, but I was just so bored out of my head, and you looked so funny!"

Mr. Baker was very angry, but he needed someone to watch his sheep because he had so many other chores to do. He warned Michael not to play the same trick again.

After a few more days, however, Michael grew even more bored than before. He looked at the cell phone lying on the ground next to him. He thought about how funny Mr. Baker looked when he found out Michael had played a trick on him. Then Michael picked up the cell phone and played the same trick again.

This time, Mr. Baker was even angrier. He told Michael that if he ever played that trick again, he would lose his job. Michael promised he wouldn't trick Mr. Baker again.

A week later, Michael was sitting under a tree watching the sheep. Out of the corner of his eye, he saw something creeping toward a sheep on the edge of the flock. Michael shaded his eyes against the bright sun. He saw that the creeping animal was a coyote. Then he saw three more. As he watched in horror, the coyotes attacked the poor sheep. The sheep went down with a terrible bleating cry. The rest of the sheep started to run.

With trembling fingers, Michael dialed Mr. Baker's number on the cell phone. When the rancher answered, Michael cried, "Mr. Baker! Come quick! A pack of coyotes is attacking the sheep!"

However, Michael heard only silence on the other end of the line. Finally, the rancher said, "I'm disappointed in you, Michael. You promised that you wouldn't do this again. I have no choice but to—"

"But Mr. B—"

"You heard me, Michael," said the rancher. "Today will be your last day working for me." Then Mr. Baker hung up.

Moral: No one will believe a liar, even when he is telling the truth.

USING the Rubric for Assessment

Go to pages 80–81 in the **Practice the Strategy Notebook!** Use that rubric to assess Brian's fable. Try using the rubric to assess your own writing.

NARRATIVE writing

Mystery

In this chapter, you will practice another kind of narrative writing: the **mystery**.

In a **mystery**, the writer creates a story about a puzzling event or crime. Both the characters and the reader try to solve the puzzle using clues that the author places in the story. Usually, at the end of the mystery, all the clues are explained, and the puzzle is solved.

The story on the next three pages is a mystery. Study the following questions. Then read the mystery, keeping the questions in mind.

 Has the writer chosen characters and a plot that appeal to the audience?

 Does the story contain clues for the characters and the reader?

 Does the writer use suspenseful words to create a feeling of mystery?

 Does all the information in the story make sense?

 Are quotations punctuated correctly?

The Case of the Disappearing Soccer Shirt

by Angela Mysterioso

"Dad! Have you seen Jacob's soccer shirt?" called Shannon. "The red and yellow one with the long sleeves?"

Shannon was searching through her brother's room and getting desperate. She had looked on the bed, under the bed, in the closet, in the dresser, on the clothes pegs, and everywhere else she could think of.

"Gee, Rufus," she said to her big, shaggy red dog. "Jake told me he would leave his shirt right on the bed so I could wear it to soccer tryouts." Shannon's older brother Jacob was a star player on the high school soccer team. Right now, he was away at soccer camp, but before he left, he had told Shannon she could wear his team shirt from last year to her tryouts.

Rufus just looked at the empty bed, where the shirt was supposed to be. Then he looked up at Shannon and wagged his tail.

Shannon's dad came into the room holding the towel he had been using to dry some dishes. "Maybe Jake decided at the last minute to take the shirt to camp with him," he suggested.

"No," answered Shannon, "I'm sure he didn't. The last thing he said before he left was that his shirt would bring me good luck at my tryouts."

Her father shrugged and said, "Well, you'll just have to look around, I guess."

"I've already looked everywhere," moaned Shannon. "Haven't I, Rufus?"

Rufus just tilted his head to the side, as if he were thinking about what Shannon had just said. Whenever he did that, he made the whole family laugh.

"It's definitely a mystery," her dad said, "but you'll find a way to solve it. Maybe Rufus can help you. In fact, helping you might even cheer him up.

I've noticed that he's been pretty unhappy since Jake went to soccer camp. All he does is hide behind the couch. I wonder why."

Shannon glanced down at her shaggy dog. "Rufus will be a huge help, I'm sure," she said with a smile. She used both hands to pull Rufus's long, tangled fur out of his eyes. "There," she said, "can you see better now? Are you ready to help me find Jake's shirt, old boy?"

"Why don't you ask Lizzie to help you, too?" Dad suggested. Lizzie was Shannon's younger sister.

"All right," answered Shannon, "but I'm not sure she'll be much help either."

A few minutes later, Lizzie eagerly joined her sister in the search for the missing shirt. Lizzie looked in the basement, poked in and around the washer and dryer, and burrowed through all the closets. Meanwhile, Shannon scoured the car and garage. She also ransacked her room, Lizzie's room, and Jake's room—again! Rufus did not offer much assistance. Mostly, he lay in a lump on the living room rug or hid behind the couch.

"I have to find that shirt really soon," Shannon reminded Lizzie. "Soccer tryouts start in three hours. If I don't find that shirt, I'll have to wear something else. I really want to wear Jake's shirt because I need all the good luck I can get at the tryouts. That shirt has got to be around here somewhere!"

Then Lizzie's eyes got big and round. "Maybe someone stole Jake's shirt!" she whispered. "I bet someone snuck in here and took it while we weren't looking!"

Shannon grinned and shook her head. "I don't think so, Lizzie, but I have to admit I don't have any better ideas right now. Anyway, Rufus would bark if a stranger came into our house." Then she spotted his tail sticking out from behind the couch. "But maybe not."

An hour later, Shannon had given up hope of locating the missing shirt. She was slouched on a kitchen chair, slowly helping her dad peel potatoes for their dinner.

Lizzie had gotten tired of searching, too, and was watching TV in the family room. She was lying on the couch, petting Rufus with her stockinged foot as she watched her favorite cartoons. "You really miss Jacob, don't you, boy?" Lizzie mumbled to the unhappy dog. "I bet that's why you didn't even notice when someone came in and stole his shirt."

Rufus got up slowly and sheepishly squeezed himself back behind the couch. After a while, Lizzie wondered how he was doing and peeped over the back of the couch. Then she let out a scream!

"Shannon! Dad! I found the thief!"

As Shannon and their dad rushed into the family room, Lizzie reached behind the couch, where Rufus was hiding. As the others watched in suspense, she pulled out the red and yellow shirt. Then Rufus crawled out from behind the couch and lay on the rug with his head on his front paws.

"Rufus had the shirt all along!" Shannon said with a sigh of relief. "Why would he take Jacob's shirt?"

"I think I know," said Dad. "Rufus really misses Jake, and dogs have a strong sense of smell. To Rufus, the shirt smells like Jake, so he pulled the shirt off the bed and carried it to his hideaway behind the couch. It probably made him feel as if Jake were nearby."

Shannon gave Rufus a warm hug, and the dog licked her face and wagged his tail. "Sorry, boy, but I need that shirt more than you do right now," she explained. "I'll give it back to you as soon as tryouts are over— I promise!"

Dad reached down and patted Rufus's head. "Why don't we take him with us to the tryouts? That way, he can keep a close watch over his favorite shirt!"

"It's everyone's favorite shirt today!" Shannon added.

Using a Rubric

A rubric is a good way to assess a piece of writing. You simply assign 1, 2, 3, or 4 points in each category in the rubric.

Remember the questions you studied on page 162? Those questions were used to make the rubric you see here.

"Hi! My name is Tia. I'm learning how to write a mystery, too. What did you think about the mystery on pages 163–165? Let's use this rubric to see how well the mystery was written. Review the questions in each category in the rubric. Next, read the scoring information for each category. Then, on pages 168–170, you and I will use this rubric to evaluate the mystery."

Has the writer chosen characters and a plot that appeal to the audience?

Does the story contain clues for the characters and the reader?

Does the writer use suspenseful words to create a feeling of mystery?

Does all the information in the story make sense?

Conventions & Skills

Are quotations punctuated correctly?

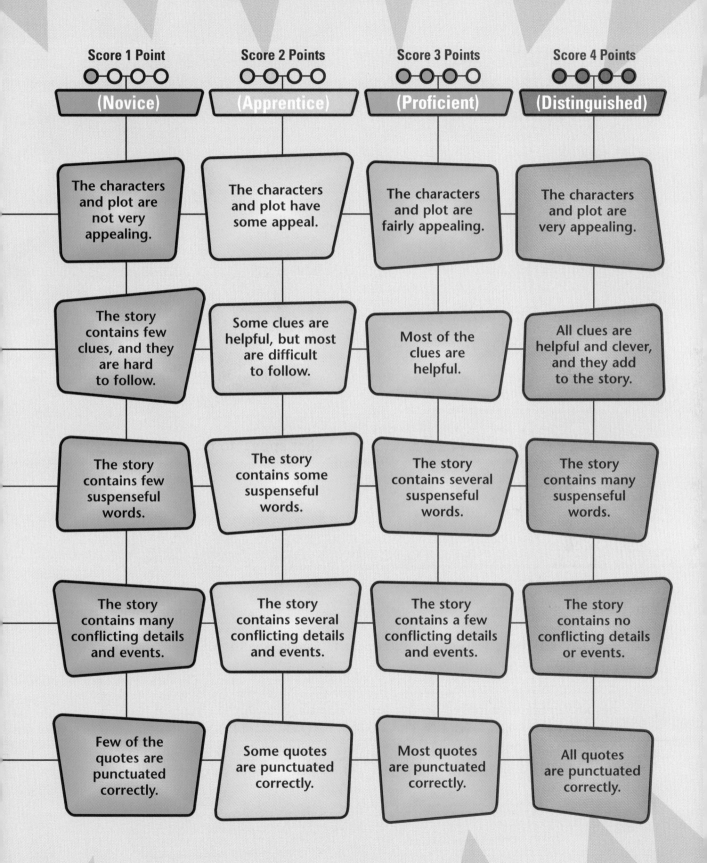

Score 1 Point	Score 2 Points	Score 3 Points	Score 4 Points
(Novice)	**(Apprentice)**	**(Proficient)**	**(Distinguished)**
The characters and plot are not very appealing.	The characters and plot have some appeal.	The characters and plot are fairly appealing.	The characters and plot are very appealing.
The story contains few clues, and they are hard to follow.	Some clues are helpful, but most are difficult to follow.	Most of the clues are helpful.	All clues are helpful and clever, and they add to the story.
The story contains few suspenseful words.	The story contains some suspenseful words.	The story contains several suspenseful words.	The story contains many suspenseful words.
The story contains many conflicting details and events.	The story contains several conflicting details and events.	The story contains a few conflicting details and events.	The story contains no conflicting details or events.
Few of the quotes are punctuated correctly.	Some quotes are punctuated correctly.	Most quotes are punctuated correctly.	All quotes are punctuated correctly.

Using a 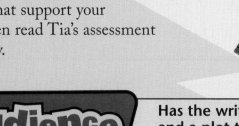 to Study the Model

Use the rubric to evaluate the mystery about the disappearing soccer shirt. Remember, you will give 1, 2, 3, or 4 points in each category.

How many points did you give the mystery? Discuss each category on the rubric with your classmates. Find words and sentences in the mystery that support your decisions. Then read Tia's assessment of the mystery.

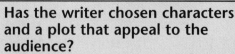 **Has the writer chosen characters and a plot that appeal to the audience?**

> Right at the beginning, the author sets up the mystery— where's the shirt? I want to know what happened to the shirt. Was it really stolen? The author also describes some very likable characters, including Rufus.

"Dad! Have you seen Jacob's soccer shirt?" called Shannon. "The red and yellow one with the long sleeves?"

Shannon was searching though her brother's room and getting desperate. She had looked on the bed, under the bed, in the closet, in the dresser, on the clothes pegs, and everywhere else she could think of.

"Gee, Rufus," she said to her big, shaggy red dog. "Jake told me he would leave his shirt right on the bed so I could wear it to soccer tryouts."

" Several clues in the story hint about what happened to the missing shirt. When you go back and reread it, you see the clues and say 'Aha!' I know one clue was that Rufus kept hiding behind the couch. Did you find other clues in the story? "

"It's definitely a mystery," her dad said, "but you'll find a way to solve it. Maybe Rufus can help you. In fact, helping you might even cheer him up. I've noticed that he's been pretty unhappy since Jake went to soccer camp. All he does is hide behind the couch. I wonder why."

 **Does the writer use suspenseful words to create a feeling of mystery?**

" This isn't really a spooky mystery, but the author works in some suspenseful words anyway. Here's one place where the author uses **sheepishly** and **scream**. **Sheepishly** made me wonder why the dog was acting like that. **Scream** made me really want to know what Lizzie saw behind the couch! "

Rufus got up slowly and sheepishly squeezed himself back behind the couch. After a while, Lizzie wondered how he was doing and peeped over the back of the couch. Then she let out a scream!

66 The author doesn't include any details or clues that conflict with each other. That would be confusing. For example, when the author tells where Shannon and Lizzie looked, she doesn't say they looked behind the couch. If they had, the mystery would be over! 99

Lizzie looked in the basement, poked in and around the washer and dryer, and burrowed through all the closets. Meanwhile, Shannon scoured the car and garage. She also ransacked her room, Lizzie's room, and Jake's room—again!

Conventions & SKILLS — Are quotations punctuated correctly?

66 It's a good thing that this author knows how to punctuate quotations. The story is full of dialogue—characters talking to each other. 99

"Why don't you ask Lizzie to help you, too?" Dad suggested. Lizzie was Shannon's younger sister.

"All right," answered Shannon, "but I'm not sure she'll be much help either."

66 **Now it's my turn to write!**

I'm going to write my own mystery. Follow along, and you will see how I use good writing strategies. I will also use the model mystery and the rubric to guide my writing. 99

Tia

Writer of a Mystery

Name: Tia
Home: Montana
Hobbies: watching old movies, playing wheelchair basketball, solving word puzzles
Hero: Christopher Reeve
Favorite Book: *The Quicksand Pony* by Alison Lester
Assignment: mystery

Prewriting

Gather
Brainstorm some people and events for my mystery.

“When our teacher asked us to write mysteries, several ideas popped into my head right away. Soon I had a whole list of possible topics and story ideas. You can see how some of them are related to my hobbies.”

Word puzzles: Write a mystery about how a word with two meanings causes problems with friends who are trying to find another friend.

Old movies: A silent screen star disappears and is never heard from until two kids find out the cause of his or her disappearance.

School: Something mysteriously appears at school and has all the kids talking.

“After looking over my notes, I decided to write a mystery about school—that's what I know best. Then I had a great idea! I would write about some mysterious posters showing up at school. What do they mean? Who put them there?”

Go to page 82 in the **Practice** the Strategy **Notebook!**

Prewriting

Organize
Make a story map to plan my mystery.

66 I know from the **Rubric** that organization is important. Now that I have decided what my story will be about, I need to think about my characters and how they solve this mystery. I will fill in a story map. It's a way to help organize my thoughts and the events in my mystery. 99

Story Map

A **story map** organizes the setting, characters, plot, problem, major events, and outcome of the story.

Setting: Place: elementary school hallways, cafeteria
Time: now

Main Characters: Erin and Torrie, fifth-grade girls

Problem/Mystery: to find out the meaning of mysterious posters and who put them up

Plot:
Event 1: Erin and Torrie see the first poster and try to figure out what it means.
Event 2: They see the second poster and are still puzzled.
Event 3: The girls see the third poster; Erin has an idea.

Outcome: Erin explains her idea to Torrie, and they find out Erin is right. The mystery is solved!

Go to page 84 in the **Practice ∧ Notebook!**
the Strategy

Drafting

Write
Draft my mystery, using the story map and paying special attention to the clues.

"Now I'll use my story map to begin drafting my mystery. The **Rubric** reminds me to pay special attention to clues. I want to give some information, so the reader has a chance to solve the puzzle along with Erin and Torrie. Still, I don't want to say too much and give the mystery away. I made the list of clues below to help me write my draft. I might change the clues as I write, though."

Clues I Want to Use

- the message on each poster
- the color of the letters
- the fact that the Drama Club is going to present a play

"The **Rubric** also says I should keep my audience in mind. I'm going to read this story to the class on Authors' Day, so I'll use words that kids usually use.

"Check out the beginning of my mystery on the next page to see what you think. I've tried to cover several different parts of my story map: setting, characters, problem, and the first event."

Those strange posters attracted a lot of attention at school. The first one appeared in the main hallway, just outside the cafeteria. When my friend Torrie and I saw it, we were talking about our two favorite subjects—old movies and what the next Drama Club play

clue → might be. We were on our way to lunch.

"Hey, erin." Torrie said. "Look at this poster. What do you think it means?

I looked at it closely. It was in bright red letters on white paper.　　clue The poster said, "Don't forget your slippers." That's it—nothing more ~~than that~~.

"Huh?" said Torrie. "Slippers at school? What's that supposed to mean? Maybe it's a new fashion trend."

I shruged my shoulders. "Beats me, I answered." Still, I couldn't stop thinking about the wierd poster for the rest of the day.

Go to page 86 in the **Practice the Strategy Notebook!**

Revising

Elaborate

Add suspenseful words. Use a thesaurus to find new words.

(READ TO A PARTNER)

"After I read my first draft to my partner, Thuy, she thought I needed to add some suspenseful words. The **Rubric** says that these words help create a feeling of mystery. I looked through my draft for words that were common and ordinary. I wanted to replace them with words that were more interesting, kind of creepy. In a thesaurus I found words that mean the same and are more suspenseful. Here are some changes I made to the next part of my mystery."

Thesaurus

A **thesaurus** is a book in which you can find synonyms (words with a similar meaning) and antonyms (words with an opposite meaning).

[2nd DRAFT]

perplexing ← **suspenseful words**

The puzzle definitely got more ~~confusing~~ the next day. Torrie and I were leaving the cafeteria after lunch when she ~~spotted~~ spied another poster.

The second poster was completely different from the first one. It was written in yellow letters and said, "Where does this road go?" A crowd of kids had gathered around it. From what they were saying, I could tell Torrie and I weren't the only ones who were ~~puzzled~~ mystified.

"I think we're in the middle of a really ~~strange~~ baffling mystery," Torrie said.

suspenseful words

Go to page 88 in the **Practice** the Strategy **Notebook!**

Revising

Clarify Check for conflicting information.

READ TO A PARTNER

❝When I read my second draft to Thuy, she liked my new suspenseful words, but she said some parts of the story didn't make sense. For example, in the part below, Erin says she knows the answer and will wait to tell Torrie what it is. Then I wrote that Erin is still thinking about the answer. That's confusing! If she knew the answer, she wouldn't still be thinking about it. Does she know it or not?

  "I rewrote that part to take out the conflicting information. It makes more sense now.❞

[3rd DRAFT]

"We need to think about the mystery the way Charlie Chan or Sherlock Holmes would," Torrie said.

She was right. Those movie detectives from the 1930s could solve any mystery.

"We need to use our heads like the scarecrow in The Wizard of Oz does after he gets a brain," she added.

revision to avoid conflicting information

~~Then I knew the answer, but I decided not to tell Torrie until the~~ Hmm, I thought to myself. Maybe Torrie had something there. ~~next day.~~ That night, I thought long and hard about the mysterious posters. Something about what Torrie said stuck in my mind, but I just couldn't come up with the right answer.

Go to page 89 in the **Practice the Strategy Notebook!**

Editing

Proofread

Check to see that I have punctuated quotations correctly.

> I've finished drafting my mystery, and now I'll check my spelling, capitalization, and punctuation, like I always do. The **Rubric** reminds me to pay special attention to how I punctuate quotes. On the next page, you can see the mistakes in punctuating quotes that I corrected in this part of my story.

Direct and Indirect Quotations

A **direct quotation** is a speaker's exact words. Use quotation marks at the beginning and end of a direct quotation. Use a comma to separate the speaker's words from the rest of the sentence. Begin a direct quotation with a capital letter and add end punctuation before the last quotation mark.

Example: Jonathan said, "I love old Hollywood movies, especially musicals."

An **indirect quotation** retells a speaker's words. Do not use quotation marks when the word *that* or *whether* comes before a speaker's words.

Example: Jonathan said that he loved old movies, especially musicals.

Extra Practice

See **Direct and Indirect Quotations** (pages CS 16–CS 17) in the back of this book.

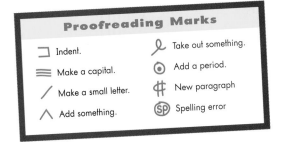

Proofreading Marks

⊐ Indent.

≡ Make a capital.

/ Make a small letter.

∧ Add something.

ℓ Take out something.

⊙ Add a period.

New paragraph

SP Spelling error

[4th DRAFT]

Those strange posters attracted a lot of attention at school. The first one appeared in the main hallway, just outside the cafeteria. When my friend Torrie and I saw it, we were talking about our two favorite subjects—old movies and what the next Drama Club play might be. We were on our way to lunch.

"Hey, Erin," Torrie said. "Look at this poster. What do you think it means?" **corrected punctuation**

I looked at it closely. It was in bright red letters on white paper. The poster said, "Don't forget your slippers." That's it—nothing more.

"Huh?" said Torrie. "Slippers at school? What's that supposed to mean? Maybe it's a new fashion trend." **corrected punctuation**

SP shrugged

I shruged my shoulders. "Beats me," I answered. Still, I couldn't

SP weird

stop thinking about the wierd poster for the rest of the day.

The puzzle definitely got more perplexing the next day. Torrie and I were leaving the cafeteria after lunch when she spied another poster.

                                    the Strategy
Go to page 90 in the **Practice** ∧ **Notebook!**

Publishing

Share
Read my mystery to the class on Authors' Day.

> **Writer:** Tia
> **Assignment:** mystery
> **Title:** "The Case of the Mysterious Posters"
> **Audience:** students
> **Method of Publication:** reading it aloud on Authors' Day
> **Reason for Choice:** to entertain the class with my mystery

"I couldn't wait for Authors' Day. I was a little nervous about reading my mystery to the class, but I was pretty sure they would like it. Besides, everyone else would be reading to the class, too. Here are the steps I followed to get ready for the big day."

1. I read my mystery to my family to see if they had any suggestions for changes. They liked it just the way it was!

2. I used our computer to make the final copy of my mystery. I knew the readers needed to see the posters, so I drew them on the pages.

3. Then I practiced reading it aloud several more times. I decided where I would pause to make the story more suspenseful and when I would hold up my posters. I even tape-recorded myself and listened to the recording to see how I sounded.

4. I got a good night's sleep before Authors' Day so I would be rested and do my best reading.

The Case of the Mysterious Posters

by Tia

Those strange posters attracted a lot of attention at school. The first one appeared in the main hallway, just outside the cafeteria. When my friend Torrie and I saw it, we were talking about our two favorite subjects—old movies and what the next Drama Club play might be. We were on our way to lunch.

"Hey, Erin," Torrie said. "Look at this poster. What do you think it means?"

I looked at it closely. It was in big bright red letters on white paper. The poster said, "Don't forget your slippers." That's it—nothing more.

"Huh?" said Torrie. "Slippers at school? What's that supposed to mean? Maybe it's a new fashion trend."

I shrugged my shoulders. "Beats me," I answered. Still, I couldn't stop thinking about the weird poster for the rest of the day.

The puzzle definitely got more perplexing the next day. Torrie and I were leaving the cafeteria after lunch when she spied another poster.

The second poster was completely different from the first. It was written in yellow letters and said, "Where does this road go?" A crowd of kids had gathered around it. From what they were saying, I could tell Torrie and I weren't the only ones mystified by the posters.

"I think we're in the middle of a really baffling mystery," Torrie said.

DON'T FORGET YOUR SLIPPERS.

WHERE DOES THIS ROAD GO?

On the bus home that day, you can imagine that the posters were all Torrie and I talked about. We traded all sorts of theories about the posters. Who was putting them up? What did they mean? Why were they so mysterious and secretive? Would another poster appear tomorrow?

"We need to think about the mystery the way Charlie Chan or Sherlock Holmes would," Torrie said.

She was right. Those movie detectives from the 1930s could solve any mystery.

"We need to use our heads like the scarecrow in *The Wizard of Oz* does after he gets a brain," she added.

Hmm, I thought to myself. Maybe Torrie had something there.

That night, I thought long and hard about the mysterious posters. Something about what Torrie said stuck in my mind, but I just couldn't come up with the right answer.

I finally drifted off to sleep, but I woke up with a start at about four in the morning. "That's it!" I cried. "That's the answer to the puzzle!"

I couldn't wait to get to school the next morning to tell Torrie what I'd figured out. I didn't see her until third period, when she came running up to me all excited.

"Guess what?" she practically yelled. "There's another poster!"

"What color are the letters?" I asked quickly.

WELCOME TO THE CITY

She looked at me as if I were crazy, and then she answered, "They're bright green. Why?"

"Then I bet the poster says something like 'Welcome to the city,'" I said with a confident smile.

Torrie's eyes almost bugged out of her head. "You—you're exactly right! How did you know?"

"You told me yesterday," I explained.

"I did? But how?" she asked.

"Remember what you said about the scarecrow in *The Wizard of Oz*? And remember how the Drama Club is trying to keep the name of its next play secret as long as it can?"

"Yes, but so what?" Torrie asked.

"Auditions are next week, right? Think about it. The first poster was about slippers and written in red letters—**ruby** red letters. The second one asked about a road and was written in yellow letters. Does a **yellow road** ring a bell? The third one welcomed us to a city in **emerald** green letters. Do these three things remind you of any old movie?" I asked.

"Well, sure," Torrie cried. "*The Wizard of Oz*! The class play is *The Wizard of Oz*!"

"Now you're using your brain, Scarecrow," I said.

Auditions NEXT WEEK for Class Play

Wizard of Oz

USING the Rubric for Assessment

Go to page 92 in the **Practice** the Strategy **Notebook!** Use that rubric to assess Tia's mystery. Try using the rubric to assess your own writing.

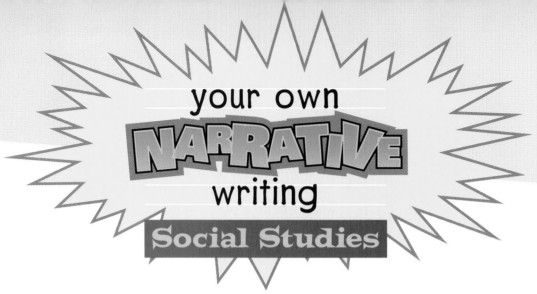

your own
NARRATIVE
writing
Social Studies

Put the strategies you practiced in this unit to work to write your own fable, mystery, or both! You can:

- develop the writing you did in the Your Own Writing pages of the *Practice the Strategy Notebook*;

- pick an idea below and write something new;

- choose another idea of your own.

Be sure to follow the steps in the writing process. Use the rubrics in this unit to assess your writing.

Fable	Mystery
• a fable set in another country • a fable set in another time period • a fable about an important event in United States history • a fable about an important event in your state	• a mystery involving a famous person • a mystery about a famous place in the world • a mystery about traveling back in history • a mystery about an event in history

portfolio

School–Home Connection

Keep a writing portfolio. Think about adding the activities from the *Practice the Strategy Notebook* to your writing portfolio. You may want to take your portfolio home to share.

PERSUASIVE writing

tries to convince the reader of something.

1

Book Review

2

Letter to the Editor

PERSUASIVE
writing

Book Review

In this chapter, you will practice one kind of persuasive writing: a **book review**.

In a **book review,** the writer presents his or her opinion about a book and tries to persuade, or convince, readers this opinion is correct. A book review is one kind of persuasive essay.

The selection on the next page is a book review. Study the following questions. Then read the book review, keeping the questions in mind.

Does the writer begin by clearly explaining his or her opinion to the audience?

Does the writer organize the review around the book's theme, characters, plot, and setting?

Does the writer include quotations and examples to support his or her opinion?

Does the writer clearly restate his or her opinion at the end of the review?

Do all pronouns have clear antecedents? Do the pronouns agree with their antecedents in number?

And Now Miguel
by Joseph Krumgold

reviewed by Sharla Baker

How does a young person prove that he or she is ready for adult responsibilities? This question is the theme of *And Now Miguel* by Joseph Krumgold. This Newbery Award-winning novel is about 12-year-old Miguel Chavez. Miguel himself tells the story. The reader sees everything through his eyes. It is a powerful tale that I strongly recommend.

Miguel and his family live on a sheep ranch in New Mexico. The boy's goal is to join the men of his family when they take the sheep to their summer pasture. The pasture is high in the mountains. Miguel wants to prove that he is ready to share this important responsibility. The story of how he proves it takes place over a year. The setting of majestic mountains adds much to the story.

I felt that the book's greatest strength is its characters. They are interesting and true to life. Miguel's family includes his older brother Gabriel, whom he admires. A younger brother is named Pedro. A secret that Miguel tells Pedro causes serious problems during the story. Another interesting character is Uncle Eli, a wise, old teacher.

The ways the characters reacted to the plot's events seemed realistic. I also liked how the book showed both good and bad events in their lives. Miguel describes "how the worst thing happened, and then how the best thing happened, and then how everything got mixed up."

On the other hand, the novel seemed a little long. I also found that the dialogue sometimes sounded phony. Overall, however, *And Now Miguel* is an exciting story of a boy becoming a man. All young people—boys and girls—should read it.

Using a **Rubric**

A rubric is a good way to assess a piece of writing. Rubrics are easy to use. You simply assign 1, 2, 3, or 4 points in each category in the rubric.

Remember the questions you studied on page 186? Those questions were used to make the rubric you see here.

> **Hi!** My name is Jared. I'm learning how to write a book review, too. What did you think of the review on page 187? Let's use this rubric to see how well it was written. Review the questions in each category in the rubric. Next, read the scoring information for each category. Then on pages 190–192, you and I will use this rubric to evaluate the book review.

Audience

Does the writer begin by clearly explaining his or her opinion to the audience?

Organization

Does the writer organize the review around the book's theme, characters, plot, and setting?

Elaboration

Does the writer include quotations and examples to support his or her opinion?

Clarification

Does the writer clearly restate his or her opinion at the end of the review?

Conventions & Skills

Do all pronouns have clear antecedents? Do the pronouns agree with their antecedents in number?

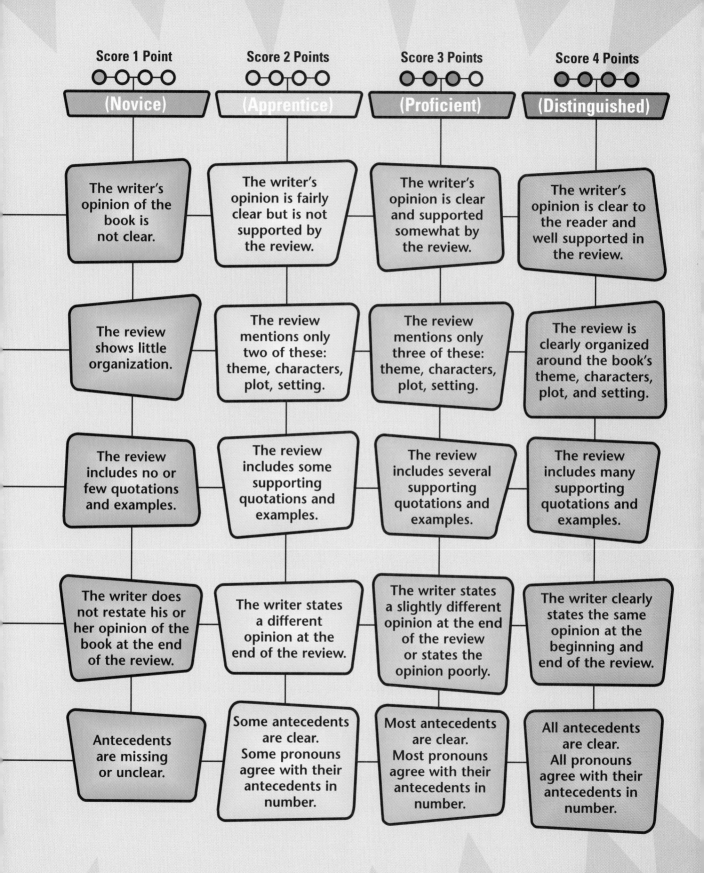

Score 1 Point
(Novice)

The writer's opinion of the book is not clear.

The review shows little organization.

The review includes no or few quotations and examples.

The writer does not restate his or her opinion of the book at the end of the review.

Antecedents are missing or unclear.

Score 2 Points
(Apprentice)

The writer's opinion is fairly clear but is not supported by the review.

The review mentions only two of these: theme, characters, plot, setting.

The review includes some supporting quotations and examples.

The writer states a different opinion at the end of the review.

Some antecedents are clear. Some pronouns agree with their antecedents in number.

Score 3 Points
(Proficient)

The writer's opinion is clear and supported somewhat by the review.

The review mentions only three of these: theme, characters, plot, setting.

The review includes several supporting quotations and examples.

The writer states a slightly different opinion at the end of the review or states the opinion poorly.

Most antecedents are clear. Most pronouns agree with their antecedents in number.

Score 4 Points
(Distinguished)

The writer's opinion is clear to the reader and well supported in the review.

The review is clearly organized around the book's theme, characters, plot, and setting.

The review includes many supporting quotations and examples.

The writer clearly states the same opinion at the beginning and end of the review.

All antecedents are clear. All pronouns agree with their antecedents in number.

Using a **Rubric** to Study the Model

Use the rubric to evaluate the book review of *And Now Miguel*. Remember, you will give 1, 2, 3, or 4 points in each category.

How many points did you give the book review? Discuss each category on the rubric with your classmates. Find words and sentences in the book review that support your decisions. Then read Jared's assessment of the book review.

**Audience**

Does the writer begin by clearly explaining his or her opinion to the audience?

❝ In the first paragraph of her review, the writer introduces the book and gives her opinion of it. Just read the last sentence below and you will know exactly what she thinks. ❞

How does a young person prove that he or she is ready for adult responsibilities? This question is the theme of *And Now Miguel* by Joseph Krumgold. This Newbery Award-winning novel is about 12-year-old Miguel Chavez. Miguel himself tells the story. The reader sees everything through his eyes. It is a powerful tale that I strongly recommend.

Organization

Does the writer organize the review around the book's theme, characters, plot, and setting?

" This writer covers all four parts of the book. You just read how she explains the theme in her first paragraph. In her next paragraph, she describes the plot and the setting. In the paragraph below, she tells about the characters. "

I felt that the book's greatest strength is its characters. They are interesting and true to life. Miguel's family includes his older brother Gabriel, whom he admires. A younger brother is named Pedro. A secret that Miguel tells Pedro causes serious problems during the story. Another interesting character is Uncle Eli, a wise, old teacher.

Elaboration

Does the writer include quotations and examples to support his or her opinion?

" In this paragraph, the writer uses a quotation from the story to illustrate one of the book's strengths: its true-to-life characters. Reading this quotation also helped me get the flavor of the novel. "

I also liked how the book showed both good and bad events in their lives. Miguel describes "how the worst thing happened, and then how the best thing happened, and then how everything got mixed up."

Clarification — Does the writer clearly restate his or her opinion at the end of the review?

> In the last paragraph, the writer mentions two weaknesses of the book but still urges people to read it. There is no doubt that she liked this story. After reading her review, I think I would, too.

On the other hand, the novel seemed a little long. I also found that the dialogue sometimes sounded phony. Overall, however, *And Now Miguel* is an exciting story of a boy becoming a man. All young people—boys and girls—should read it.

Conventions & Skills — Do all pronouns have clear antecedents? Do the pronouns agree with their antecedents in number?

> The writer made sure that all pronouns agree with their antecedents in number. In the very first paragraph, for example, she is careful with a tricky antecedent. Because a **young person** is singular, the writer has to use **he** or **she** as the pronoun, not **they**.

How does a young person prove that he or she is ready for adult responsibilities? This question is the theme of *And Now Miguel* by Joseph Krumgold.

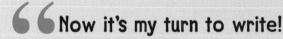 **Now it's my turn to write!**

> I'm going to write my own book review. Follow along, and you will see how I use good writing strategies. I will also use the model book review and the rubric to guide my writing.

JARED

Writer of a Book Review

Name:	Jared
Home:	California
Hobbies:	reading about history, mountain biking, camping
Favorite Food:	anything cooked over a campfire!
Assignment:	book review

Prewriting

Gather

As I read my book, take notes on ideas I might include in my review.

"After my teacher, Mrs. Summers, asked us to write a book review, I just couldn't find a book that seemed interesting. Then Mrs. Summers suggested The Arrow Over the Door by Joseph Bruchac. One of the main characters is a Quaker. I had mentioned in class one day that I am a Quaker, and Mrs. Summers remembered!

"The book is based on a real event that happened during the American Revolution. After I read the jacket copy, I really wanted to read the book. As I read, I took notes about ideas I might want to use in my review."

Notes on The Arrow Over the Door
by Joseph Bruchac

- Story takes place in 1777 during the Revolutionary War near Saratoga, (upstate) NY.

- Samuel Russell is young Quaker boy.

- Stands Straight is Abenaki Indian boy.

- Story is told from each boy's point of view.

- Theme: each boy learns about himself, his own strengths, and his people's beliefs.

- Plot follows Quakers and Indians until they finally meet.

- Story contains much interesting information about Quaker and Abenaki traditions and beliefs.

Go to page 94 in the **Practice** the Strategy **Notebook!**

Prewriting

Organize
Use my notes to make a pros-and-cons chart.

66 After reviewing my notes, I decided to make a pros-and-cons chart. It will help me figure out what I liked and disliked about The Arrow Over the Door. A pros-and-cons chart can also help me make sure I cover the book's theme, characters, plot, and setting, like the **Rubric** suggests. 99

Pros-and-Cons Chart

A **pros-and-cons chart** shows the positive points (pros) and negative points (cons) about a topic or issue.

	Pros (what I liked)	Cons (what I disliked)
Plot	Two people tell a story, and the stories come together at the end.	Book ended too soon; I wanted to know what the boys did as the war continued.
Theme	Each boy questions his own beliefs but comes to understand them better.	
Setting	The author uses the setting—upstate New York—to show the loneliness but also the friendliness of the wilderness.	
Characters	I learned how the two boys are similar and different.	
Language	The author made the Abenaki and Quaker speech different.	
Other	I learned interesting details about Quakers and Abenakis; the author himself is Abenaki.	Author could have told more about some of the other characters.

Go to page 96 in the **Practice** the Strategy **Notebook!**

Drafting

Write
Draft my book review, starting with my thesis statement.

“Now I'm ready to write. The **Rubric** reminds me to start with my opinion of the book, which is my thesis statement. A quick glance at my pros-and-cons chart showed that I liked the book much more than I disliked it. It was really a good story!

“As I thought about why I liked this book, I realized that the main reason was its theme, the author's message to us readers. The two boys came from much different backgrounds but wondered about the same things. Sometimes I wonder about the same things they did, especially why people go to war. It was interesting to find out how they answered these questions.

“On the next page, you can see how I started my review with my thesis statement. Having a thesis statement made writing the rest of the review much easier. I just had to keep giving reasons why I liked the book, especially its theme.”

Thesis Statement

A **thesis statement** is the writer's opinion. In an essay or book review, the writer presents points to try to convince the reader that his or her thesis statement is correct.

The Arrow Over the Door
by Joseph Bruchac
reviewed by Jared

Two boys, an American Quaker named Samuel Russell and an Abenaki Indian named Stands Straight, are the main characters in this ^historical^ novel by Joseph Bruchac. The boys are from very different backgrounds. ^However,^ When they meet, they learn about themselves and about other people's fears, hopes, and beliefs. I really liked this book because I could identify with how the boys tried to sort out their feelings and beliefs and better understand them.

thesis statement

The story is told from each boy's point of view. Readers get to know each character's thoughts ^and feelings^. We find out ways they are similar and ~~other~~ ways they are different. The story takes place during the American Revolution. The setting is upstate New york.

Go to page 98 in the **Practice** ^the Strategy^ **Notebook!**

Revising

Elaborate

Include quotations and examples to support my opinion.

> When I read my first draft, I got the feeling something was missing. Then I remembered that the Rubric says to add quotations and examples to support my thesis statement. Adding quotations and examples will also help the reader get a feeling for the novel and the author's style of writing.
>
> "Below is one change I made. I had explained in my first draft that the Quaker characters and the Abenaki characters talked differently, but I didn't give an example. In my second draft, I added a quotation to show the kind of language the Quaker characters use.

READ TO MYSELF

[2nd DRAFT]

added quotation

The language of the characters adds richness to the story. For example, Samuel's parents know that he is worried. "What is troubling thy heart, Samuel?" his mother asks. Samuel is concerned about how his peace-loving family will react to the battle that will soon take place.

added example

Go to page 99 in the **Practice** the Strategy **Notebook!**

Persuasive Writing · Book Review

Revising

Clarify
Restate my opinion at the end of the book review.

> When I was almost finished with my book review, I checked the **Rubric** one more time. That's when I discovered I had forgotten to restate my opinion at the end of my review! In fact, I ended it by talking about the weaknesses of the book. That would sure discourage people from reading it.
>
> "I decided to add another short paragraph to my review. I reminded readers that I really liked the book and they probably would, too.

[3rd DRAFT]

I have only a few criticisms of the novel. Some readers may feel that the author focuses too closely on the two main characters. He was interesting, but I would have liked to know more about some of the other characters. I was especially interested in the Quaker visitor Robert Nisbet and the Abenaki leader Sees-the-Wind. Other readers may agree with us that the book seems to finish too soon. I wanted to know more about what happened to Samuel and Stands Straight as the Revolutionary War continued.

Overall, however, The Arrow Over the Door is an excellent novel. I recommend it strongly for anyone who wants to read an exciting and interesting historical novel. ◄── **restated opinion**

Go to page 100 in the **Practice** the Strategy **Notebook!**

Editing

Proofread

Make sure pronoun antecedents are clear. Check to see that pronouns agree with their antecedents in number.

" All right! That last change really helped. Now I'm ready to proofread my book review. Like I always do, I'll check my spelling, capitalization, and punctuation. I also need to make sure that each pronoun has a clear antecedent and that each pronoun agrees with its antecedent in number.

"On the next page, you'll see some of the mistakes I corrected while I was proofreading my review. "

Pronouns and Antecedents

A **pronoun** is a word that replaces a noun. An **antecedent** is the word or phrase that a pronoun replaces. The antecedent of each pronoun should be clear to the reader.

Unclear: Stands Straight told Samuel **he** was wrong.
(Does *he* refer to Stands Straight or Samuel?)
Clear: Stands Straight said, "**I** am wrong, Samuel."
(Stands Straight is talking, so *I* refers to Stands Straight.)

Pronouns must agree with their antecedents in number. A singular antecedent requires a singular pronoun. A plural antecedent requires a plural pronoun.

Incorrect: When a **Quaker** goes to a meeting, **they** mostly remain silent. (*Quaker* is singular, but *they* is plural.)
Correct: When **Quakers** go to a meeting, **they** mostly remain silent. (*Quakers* and *they* are both plural.)

Extra Practice

See **Pronouns and Antecedents** (pages CS 18–CS 19) in the back of this book.

Proofreading Marks

⊐ Indent.

≡ Make a capital.

/ Make a small letter.

∧ Add something.

ℓ Take out something.

⊙ Add a period.

New paragraph

SP Spelling error

[4th DRAFT]

The author's use of setting is ~~especialy~~ especially interesting. To both Samuel and Stands straight, the wilderness is a place where ~~he~~ they can look for answers to ~~his~~ their most puzzling questions. In one scene, Samuel look**s** into a sparkling brook at ~~their~~ his reflection. He feels unhappy and confused about his life and future⊙ "He stared at it, wondering how another face might look," writes Bruchac. In another scene, Stands Straight prays to Elder Brother Sun. "I asked our Elder Brother if it is really war that ~~they~~ he want**s** for us."

I have only a few criticisms of the novel. Some readers may feel that the author focuses too closely on the two main characters. ~~He~~ They were ~~was~~ interesting, but I would have liked to know more about some of the other characters. I was especially interested in the Quaker visitor Robert Nisbet and the Abenaki leader Sees-the-Wind. Other readers may agree with ~~us~~ me that the book seems to finish too soon. I wanted to know more about what happened to Samuel and Stands Straight as the Revolutionary War continued.

pronoun matches antecedent

pronoun matches antecedent

Go to page 101 in the **Practice** the Strategy **Notebook!**

Publishing

Share — Submit my book review to a literary magazine.

Writer:	Jared
Assignment:	book review
Topic:	review of *The Arrow Over the Door* by Joseph Bruchac
Audience:	student readers of the school district's literary magazine
Method of Publication:	publish in a literary magazine
Reason for Choice:	to encourage other students to read the novel

"I thought that other students might want to know about this novel, so I decided to send my review to our school district's literary magazine. This magazine publishes stories, poems, essays, book reviews, and other work by students like me. Here's what I did to submit my book review to the magazine."

1. First, I typed a neat, double-spaced copy of my review.

2. Then I wrote a cover letter to the magazine editor. In the letter, I explained a little about myself and why I was submitting my book review to the magazine.

3. I addressed an envelope and put my letter and my review in it.

4. Last, I put a stamp on the envelope and mailed it.

The Arrow Over the Door
by Joseph Bruchac
reviewed by Jared

Two boys, an American Quaker named Samuel Russell and an Abenaki Indian named Stands Straight, are the main characters in this historical novel by Joseph Bruchac. The boys are from very different backgrounds. However, when they meet, they learn about themselves and about other people's fears, hopes, and beliefs. I really liked this book because I could identify with how the boys tried to sort out their feelings and beliefs and better understand them.

The story is told from each boy's point of view. Readers get to know each character's thoughts and feelings. We find out ways they are similar and ways they are different. The story takes place during the American Revolution. The setting is upstate New York.

A battle is coming. Samuel doubts that the Quakers' belief in nonviolence will be able to keep them from harm. Should he use a weapon to defend his people if danger approaches? The book focuses on his struggle to understand the beliefs of his Quaker people.

At the same time, Stands Straight questions the Abenakis' part in the war. Why have their leaders decided to fight for King George and against the Americans? They will be fighting people they do not know. How can he bring himself to make war against the young white boy? Samuel seems almost like his brother.

The two boys' beliefs are well described by the author, who is an Abenaki. He has also researched the beliefs and actions of Quakers during the Revolutionary War. Bruchac's understanding of the two cultures is part of what makes this book special.

The language of the characters adds richness to the story. For example, Samuel's parents know that the boy is worried. "What is troubling thy heart, Samuel?" his mother asks. Samuel is concerned about how his peace-loving family will react to the battle that will soon take place.

The author's use of setting is especially interesting. To both Samuel and Stands Straight, the wilderness is a place where they can look for answers to their most puzzling questions. In one scene, Samuel looks into a sparkling brook at his reflection. He feels unhappy and

Persuasive Writing • Book Review

confused about his life and future. "He stared at it, wondering how another face might look," writes Bruchac. In another scene, Stands Straight prays to Elder Brother Sun. "I asked our Elder Brother if it is really war that he wants for us."

I have only a few criticisms of the novel. Some readers may feel that the author focuses too closely on the two main characters. They were interesting, but I would have liked to know more about some of the other characters. I was especially interested in the Quaker visitor Robert Nisbet and the Abenaki leader Sees-the-Wind. Other readers may agree with me that the book seems to finish too soon. I wanted to know more about what happened to Samuel and Stands Straight as the Revolutionary War continued.

Overall, however, *The Arrow Over the Door* is an excellent novel. I recommend it strongly for anyone who wants to read an exciting and interesting historical novel.

USING the Rubric for Assessment

Go to pages 102–103 in the **Practice the Strategy Notebook!** Use that rubric to assess Jared's book review. Try using the rubric to assess your own writing.

PERSUASIVE writing

Letter to the Editor

In this chapter, you will practice another kind of persuasive writing: a **letter to the editor.**

In a **letter to the editor,** the writer gives an opinion and tries to persuade, or convince, readers that this opinion is correct. Then the writer sends the letter to the editor of a newspaper or magazine. If the letter is printed, many people will read it. This kind of letter is written in a business letter format.

On the next page is a letter to the editor. Study the following questions. Then read the letter, keeping the questions in mind.

 **Audience** Does the writer focus on a topic that will interest the readers?

 **Organization** Does the writer organize his or her reasons from most important to least important?

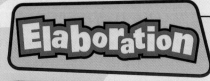 **Elaboration** Does the writer support his or her opinions with reasons and facts?

 **Clarification** Does the writer use signal words to clarify his or her ideas?

 **Conventions & Skills** Does the writer include all six parts of a business letter and avoid sentence fragments?

LETTER TO THE EDITOR · MODEL

heading — 114 Essex Street
Northville, OH 430—
October 16, 20—

Editor, *Northville Gazette*
1455 Washington Boulevard — inside address
Northville, OH 430—

Dear Editor: ← salutation

body

I am writing to address a serious problem. It is the lack of a town recycling program. Many cities and towns around the nation have recycling programs. Yet our town is one of the few without one. We are missing a great chance to save energy. We could also be lowering pollution and cutting down on the amount of trash going to our landfills. In addition, we could earn money for important community programs.

The most important reason to recycle is to save energy by reusing materials. Did you know that just five recycled plastic bottles provide enough filling for one ski jacket? Did you know that recycling a ton of paper saves 7,000 gallons of water? This water would have been used to produce new paper.

Did you know that recycling just one aluminum can saves energy? It is enough energy to run a computer for three hours! Did you know that recycling just one glass bottle can save energy? This energy can power a 100-watt light bulb for four hours!

When we conserve energy, power plants need to produce less energy. As a result, there is less pollution in our air. When we reuse materials, we send less trash to landfills. Finally, our town can sell the materials we recycle. In this way, we can earn money for programs we need and want.

Nearly 90 percent of all Americans recycle. However, our community does not. In fact, a recycling program could be run by volunteers, perhaps with a paid coordinator. Who knows how many valuable resources we are throwing away every day? Now is the time to take this important step toward saving our environment and improving our community!

Sincerely, ← closing

Cody Allen ← signature
Cody Allen

Using a Rubric

A rubric is a good way to assess a piece of writing. It can also help you plan and organize your own writing. To use a rubric, you simply assign 1, 2, 3, or 4 points in each category in the rubric.

Remember the questions you studied on page 206? Those questions were used to make the rubric you see here.

> Hi! My name is Halle. I'm learning how to write a letter to the editor, too. What did you think about the letter on page 207? Let's use this rubric to see how well the letter was written. Review the questions in each category in the rubric. Next, read the scoring information for each category. Then, on pages 210–212, you will use this rubric to evaluate the letter to the editor.

Audience

Does the writer focus on a topic that will interest the readers?

Organization

Does the writer organize his or her reasons from most important to least important?

Elaboration

Does the writer support his or her opinions with reasons and facts?

Clarification

Does the writer use signal words to clarify his or her ideas?

Conventions & Skills

Does the writer include all six parts of a business letter and avoid sentence fragments?

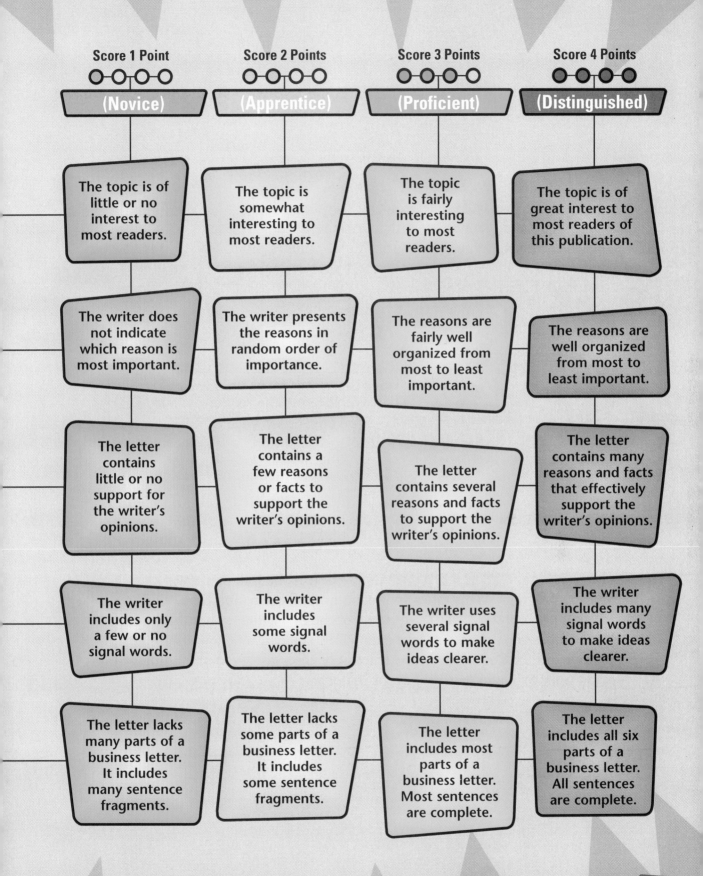

Score 1 Point	Score 2 Points	Score 3 Points	Score 4 Points
(Novice)	**(Apprentice)**	**(Proficient)**	**(Distinguished)**
The topic is of little or no interest to most readers.	The topic is somewhat interesting to most readers.	The topic is fairly interesting to most readers.	The topic is of great interest to most readers of this publication.
The writer does not indicate which reason is most important.	The writer presents the reasons in random order of importance.	The reasons are fairly well organized from most to least important.	The reasons are well organized from most to least important.
The letter contains little or no support for the writer's opinions.	The letter contains a few reasons or facts to support the writer's opinions.	The letter contains several reasons and facts to support the writer's opinions.	The letter contains many reasons and facts that effectively support the writer's opinions.
The writer includes only a few or no signal words.	The writer includes some signal words.	The writer uses several signal words to make ideas clearer.	The writer includes many signal words to make ideas clearer.
The letter lacks many parts of a business letter. It includes many sentence fragments.	The letter lacks some parts of a business letter. It includes some sentence fragments.	The letter includes most parts of a business letter. Most sentences are complete.	The letter includes all six parts of a business letter. All sentences are complete.

Using a Rubric
to Study the Model

Use the rubric to evaluate the letter about recycling.
How many points did you give this letter to the editor?
Discuss each category on the rubric with your classmates. Find
words and sentences in the letter that support your evaluation.
Then read Halle's assessment of this letter.

Does the writer focus on a topic that will interest the readers?

"Yes, this topic directly affects the readers of this newspaper. Look at the way the writer starts out her letter by clearly explaining why the issue is important to people in her town."

I am writing to address a serious problem. It is the lack of a town recycling program. Many cities and towns around the nation have recycling programs. Yet our town is one of the few without one. We are missing a great chance to save energy. We could also be lowering pollution and cutting down on the amount of trash going to our landfills. In addition, we could earn money for important community programs.

❝ This writer clearly states her most important reason to recycle: to save energy. She devotes two whole paragraphs to that reason, as you can see below. In the next paragraph, she mentions the less important reasons. She describes each of them in one or two sentences. It's easy to tell which reason she thinks is most important, isn't it? ❞

The most important reason to recycle is to save energy by reusing materials. Did you know that just five recycled plastic bottles provide enough filling for one ski jacket? Did you know that recycling a ton of paper saves 7,000 gallons of water? This water would have been used to produce new paper.

Did you know that recycling just one aluminum can saves energy? It is enough energy to run a computer for three hours! Did you know that recycling just one glass bottle can save energy? This energy can power a 100-watt light bulb for four hours!

When we conserve energy, power plants need to produce less energy. As a result, there is less pollution in our air. When we reuse materials, we send less trash to landfills. Finally, our town can sell the materials we recycle. In this way, we can earn money for programs we need and want.

Does the writer support his or her opinions with reasons and facts?

❝ I noticed in the first two paragraphs above how the writer doesn't just say that recycling saves energy and leave it at that. She gives specific facts to show how recycling saves energy and reuses materials. I thought it was interesting how she presents these facts as questions, starting each one with **Did you know. . .** ❞

Clarification

Does the writer use signal words to clarify his or her ideas?

> She sure does. In her first paragraph, the writer uses the signal words **Yet** and **In addition**. She repeats **Did you know** in the second and third paragraphs to alert readers that an important piece of information is coming. Look at how she uses **However** and **In fact** in her last paragraph to help the ideas flow smoothly together.

Nearly 90 percent of all Americans recycle. However, our community does not. In fact, a recycling program could be run by volunteers, perhaps with a paid coordinator.

Conventions & Skills

Does the writer include all six parts of a business letter and avoid sentence fragments?

> The letter includes all six parts of a business letter: the heading, inside address, salutation, body, closing, and signature. In addition, every sentence has both a subject and a verb, so there are no sentence fragments. Can you find the subject and the verb in the sentence below?

Now is the time to take this important step toward saving our environment and improving our community!

Now it's my turn to write!

> I'm going to write my own letter to the editor. Follow along, and you will see how I use good writing strategies. I will also use the model letter and the rubric to guide my writing.

HaLLE

Writer of a
Letter to the Editor

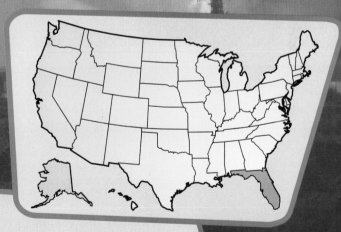

Name:	Halle
Home:	Florida
Favorite Clothes:	old jeans my big sister used to wear
Hobby:	taking care of my dog, two cats, gerbil, and parrot
Favorite Book:	*The Incredible Journey* by Sheila Burnford
Assignment:	letter to the editor

Prewriting

Gather
Use what I read and learn from others to form an opinion about a topic.

" I love pets! That's why I got so upset when I learned that our local animal shelter is in big trouble. The people who work and volunteer there have way too much to do. The staff really cares about animals—like I do—but they don't get enough money or help. I decided something had to be done!

"First, I wanted to learn as much as I could about animal shelters. I found some good newspaper and magazine articles at the library. The librarian helped me find some information on the Internet, and I talked to people at the local shelter. Here are some of the notes I took on what I learned. "

Opinion

An **opinion** is a belief, often strong, that cannot be proven to be true.

My Notes About the Local Animal Shelter

* The shelter finds homes for animals, provides shelter for strays, helps people find lost pets, educates people about owning pets, helps control rabies and other diseases, and investigates pet abuse and neglect.
* The shelter is understaffed. Cages get cleaned only once a week. Animals get little time outside their cages.
* The shelter needs volunteers to care for and play with the animals, help get animals ready for adoption, clean cages and play areas, raise money, talk to school classes about the shelter, answer telephones, and do many other tasks.

Go to page 104 in the **Practice** the Strategy **Notebook!**

Persuasive Writing • Letter to the Editor

PrewRiting

Organize
Make an outline to focus and support my opinion.

" After reading over my notes on the animal shelter, I decided to write a letter to the editor of our local newspaper. I will encourage the people in our town, especially the kids, to volunteer at the shelter and help make it a great place for animals and people.

"The **Rubric** reminds me to organize my reasons from most important to least important. I decided to use an outline to do that. I've got three main points. They'll be the Roman numerals I., II., and III. I'll make I. my most important reason. "

I. The shelter provides important services.
   A. It finds homes for animals.
   B. It helps people find lost pets.
   C. It helps control rabies and other diseases.
   D. The staff investigates pet abuse and neglect.
II. Staff is working hard, but there aren't enough people.
   A. There is only one staff person for every 40 animals.
   B. Cages get cleaned only once a week.
   C. Animals do not get much play time.
III. Community is not helping enough with money.
   A. Shelter needs more equipment and supplies.
   B. Our town spends more on holiday decorations than on the animal shelter.

Outline

An **outline** shows the main points or reasons and supporting details or facts in a piece of writing. Each main point or reason should have a Roman numeral. Each supporting detail should have a capital letter. An outline can be written in sentences or phrases—but not a combination of both.

Go to page 106 in the **Practice** the Strategy **Notebook!**

Drafting

Write

Draft my letter to the editor. State my opinion, support it, and sum up my argument.

"I want my letter to convince readers to help the animal shelter, so I have to make sure that it gets my message across to them. In my first paragraph, I'll explain my opinion. The next paragraphs will include reasons why the community should support the shelter. I'll use my outline to write that part.

"Then my last paragraph will sum up my argument. It will also suggest ways that kids can help the shelter. I really hope my letter makes a difference!

"You can read my first draft on the next page. As I drafted my letter, I did my best with spelling and grammar. I just wanted to get my ideas down on paper. I'll go back and check for mistakes later."

Dear Editor,
                         Almost no one   sp mistreat
   Few people in our community would misstreat a cat or dog.

Ignoring animals can lead to harm and suffering. Our community has

a shelter to take care of these animals. It needs our help. We must
              important
support the activities of our town's Animal shelter. ⟵——— **writer's
                                                              opinion**

   The animals shelter provides many services to the pets in our com-⌉
                                                              Reason I
munity. It helps in many important ways.   ⌋

   This shelter is staffed by dedicated workers. They cant do it all.⌉

Needs your financial help as well as your help, time and energy. Kids|
                                                              Reason II
especially can pitch in as volunters.   ⌋

   This town needs to provide more financial support, too. The shelter⌉
                                                              Reason III
needs more equipment and supplies. Our town can afford it.   ⌋

   Our community is good and caring. We must make sure this caring⌉

includes our pets. The best way to do this is to support our animal|

shelter. Students can help by feeding and playing with the animals,|

cleaning cages, and raising money. They can also tell people about|

the shelter. Call 555-8943 to see what you can do.   ⌋

                                                              **summary of
                                                              argument**

                                        the Strategy
Go to page 108 in the **Practice ⋀ Notebook!**

Revising

Elaborate
Add reasons and facts to support my opinion.

READ TO A PARTNER

"When I read my first draft to Ivan, my partner, he pointed out that I couldn't just say that we should support the shelter because it provides important services. He thought my letter would be stronger if I added more reasons and facts.

"Ivan was right. I had more reasons and facts in my outline, but I left them out of my letter. I needed to add more facts to my letter to convince my readers to help the shelter. Here's one place in my letter where I added some facts to support my opinion. I think the change makes my letter more persuasive. What do you think?"

Reason
A **reason** is the explanation behind an act, idea, or argument. For example, one reason to wear a coat outdoors is that the temperature is only 40 degrees.

[2nd DRAFT]

The animals shelter provides many services to the pets in our community. ~~It helps in many important ways.~~

The shelter finds homes for animals, helps people find lost pets, helps control rabbies and other diseases, and investigates pet abuse and neglect.   ⎤ added facts

Go to page 110 in the **Practice** the Strategy **Notebook!**

Persuasive Writing • Letter to the Editor

Revising

Clarify   Add signal words to clarify my ideas.

"Ivan also reminded me that the **Rubric** says to include signal words. Signal words act like road signs. They show what's coming next and how ideas are linked together. They will make my letter easier to understand.

"I added some signal words to these two paragraphs. I think they will help readers understand my ideas."

Signal Words

Signal words help tie ideas together. They signal that the writer is moving from one idea to the next, making an important point, comparing or contrasting ideas, or coming to the conclusion. Here are some signal words and phrases: *in the same way, also, on the other hand, although, yet, but, however, after, during, first, second, meanwhile, next, soon, later, finally, then, as a result, in fact, for example.*

[3rd DRAFT]

Dear Editor,

signal word

Almost no one in our community would mistreat a cat or dog.
However,
Ignoring animals can lead to harm and suffering. Our community has
, but   signal word
a shelter to take care of these animals. It needs our help. We must

support the important activities of our town's animal shelter.   signal words

signal words   The animals shelter provides many services to the pets in our com-
For example,
munity. The shelter finds homes for animals, helps people find lost
and   In addition, it
pets, helps control rabbies and other diseases. and investigates pet

abuse and neglect.

Go to page 111 in the **Practice** the Strategy **Notebook!**

Persuasive Writing • Letter to the Editor

Editing

Proofread

Check that I have written all six parts of a business letter correctly and that there are no sentence fragments.

"Now I need to check my spelling, capitalization, and punctuation. I'll also make sure I included all six parts of a business letter and punctuated them correctly. Finally, I need to check for sentence fragments.

"On the next page, you'll see part of my letter and some of the mistakes I corrected. I will add the other parts of a business letter in my final draft."

Business Letters

A letter to the editor is one kind of business letter. It contains six parts:

- the heading, which gives your address and the date
- the inside address, which gives your reader's name and address
- the salutation, followed by a colon (Dear Editor:)
- the body, or your message
- the closing, followed by a comma (Sincerely,)
- your signature, with your typed name under it

Sentence Fragments

A **complete sentence** has a subject and a verb. A **sentence fragment** is missing either a subject or a verb. It does not state a complete thought.

Sentence Fragment: Want to help stray pets.

Complete Sentence: Most Americans want to help stray pets.

Extra Practice
See **Sentence Fragments** (pages CS 20–CS 21) in the back of this book.

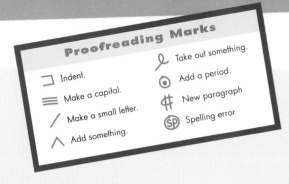

5645 Worthington ̲r̲oad
                    e
Gai̲n̲sville, FL 326—
        ∧   ∧
October 16, 20—

Editor, *TriCounty Tribune*

561 Third ̲s̲treet

Gainesville, FL 326—
           ∧
Dear Editor,
            ∧

[4th DRAFT]

corrected sentence fragment

Almost no one in our community would mistreat a cat or dog. However, ignoring animals can lead to harm and suffering. Our community has a shelter to take care of these animals, but it needs our help. We must support the important activities of our town's animal

→ The shelter is

shelter. A valuable but neglected resource in our community.
       ∧

The local animals shelter provides many services to the pets in our community. For example, the shelter finds homes for animals, helps

ⓢⓟ rabies

people find lost pets, and helps control ̶r̶a̶b̶b̶i̶e̶s̶ and other dis-
                                              ∧ All of these services ⌐
eases. In addition, it investigates pet abuse and neglect. Require
                                                          ∧
money, as well as people to carry them out.

corrected sentence fragments

This shelter is staffed by dedicated workers, but they can't do it
                                                            ∨
all. Each staff member is respo̶n̶ible for nearly 40 animals. That
                        ⓢⓟ s
                          ∧
                                                    The animals ←
means the cages get cleaned only once a week. Rarely get to play.
                                                  ∧
The staff
Needs your financial help, as well as your time and energy. Kids
∧
                                      volunteers ⓢⓟ
especially can pitch in as ̶v̶o̶l̶u̶n̶t̶e̶r̶s̶.
                             ∧

                            the Strategy
Go to page 112 in the **Practice ∧ Notebook!**

Publishing

Share   Submit my essay to a newspaper or magazine.

Writer: Halle
Assignment: letter to the editor
Topic: supporting the animal shelter
Audience: people in my town
Method of Publication: send letter to the local newspaper
Reason for Choice: make people aware that our animal shelter needs money and volunteers

" Sending my letter to the editor of our local newspaper might help other people learn about the activities and needs of our animal shelter. I've seen letters from other students in the paper, so I thought it might publish mine. Here's what I did to submit my letter to our newspaper. "

1. I used a computer to print a neat copy of the final draft. I made sure it included all six parts of a business letter.

2. Then I signed my letter above my typed name.

3. Next, I got an envelope and addressed it to the editor of our newspaper.

4. I put a stamp on the envelope and mailed it.

5645 Worthington Road
Gainesville, FL 326—
October 16, 20—

Editor, *TriCounty Tribune*
561 Third Street
Gainesville, FL 326—

Dear Editor:

Almost no one in our community would mistreat a cat or dog. However, ignoring animals can lead to harm and suffering. Our community has a shelter to take care of these animals, but it needs our help. We must support the important activities of our town's animal shelter. The shelter is a valuable but neglected resource in our community.

The animal shelter provides many important services to the pets in our community. For example, the shelter finds homes for animals, helps people find lost pets, and helps control rabies and other diseases. In addition, it investigates pet abuse and neglect. All of these services require money, as well as people to carry them out.

This shelter is staffed by dedicated workers, but they can't do it all. Each staff member is responsible for nearly 40 animals. That means the cages get cleaned only once a week. The animals rarely get to play. The staff needs your financial help, as well as your time and energy. Kids especially can pitch in as volunteers.

Our town needs to provide more financial support, too. The shelter needs more equipment and supplies. Our town can afford it. We now spend more on holiday decorations than we spend on the shelter. This must change!

Our community is good and caring. We must make sure this caring includes our pets. The best way to do this is to support our animal shelter. Students can help by feeding and playing with the animals, cleaning cages, and raising money. They can also tell people about the shelter. Call 555-8943 to see what you can do.

Sincerely,
Halle Garvin
Halle Garvin

USING the Rubric for Assessment

Go to page 114 in the **Practice** the Strategy **Notebook!** Use that rubric to assess Halle's letter to the editor. Try using the rubric to assess your own writing.

your own PERSUASIVE writing

Responding to Literature

Put the strategies you practiced in this unit to work to write your own book review, letter to the editor, or both! You can:

- develop the writing you did in the Your Own Writing pages of the *Practice the Strategy Notebook*;
- pick an idea below and write something new;
- choose another idea of your own.

Be sure to follow the steps in the writing process. Use the rubrics in this unit to assess your writing.

Book Review

- of *Hatchet* by Gary Paulsen, *Ramona Quimby* by Beverly Cleary, *My Side of the Mountain* by Jean Craighead George, or another novel
- of a poem or collection of poems
- of a biography, such as *Journey to Topaz* by Yoshiko Uchida

Letter to the Editor

- about a community issue discussed in a nonfiction book you have read
- about how a problem in your community was faced by a character in a novel
- about a biography you read that will interest your readers

portfolio

School–Home Connection

Keep a writing portfolio. Think about adding the activities from the *Practice the Strategy Notebook* to your writing portfolio. You may want to take your portfolio home to share.

TEST writing

A writing test measures how well you can organize your ideas on an assigned topic.

Test Writing

- ☑ **starts with a writing prompt.**
- ☑ **may not let writers use outside sources.**
- ☑ **may have a time limit.**
- ☑ **may not allow writers to recopy.**

TEST writing

Analyze the Writing Prompt

Every writing test starts with a writing prompt. Most writing prompts have three parts, but the parts are not always labeled. They include the Setup, the Task, and the Scoring Guide.

Read the writing prompt below carefully.

WRITING MODEL PROMPT

You have agreed to tell young children about a special skill that you have. It may be how to do or make something. Perhaps you will explain a skill you use in a hobby.

Write an explanation of the skill you choose. Explain how to do or make something. Be sure your writing

- clearly identifies the topic for your audience early in the paper.
- is well organized. You should include an introduction, body, and conclusion.
- includes details or facts that help readers understand each main idea.
- uses signal words to connect ideas.
- uses the conventions of language and spelling correctly.

Setup

This part of the writing prompt gives you the information you need to get ready to write.

You have agreed to tell young children about a special skill that you have. It may be how to do or make something. Perhaps you will explain a skill you use in a hobby.

Task

This part of the writing prompt tells you exactly what you are supposed to write: an explanation of a skill.

Write an explanation of the skill you choose. Explain how to do or make something.

Scoring Guide

This section tells how your writing will be scored. To do well on the test, you should make sure your writing does everything on the list.

Be sure your writing
- clearly identifies the topic for your audience early in the paper.
- is well organized. You should include an introduction, body, and conclusion.
- includes details or facts that help readers understand each main idea.
- uses signal words to connect ideas.
- uses the conventions of language and spelling correctly.

Using the
Scoring Guide
to Study the Model

"Hi! I'm Phanna. Like you, I sometimes take writing tests. To do well on these tests, I always pay close attention to the Scoring Guide in the writing prompt.

"Remember the rubrics you read earlier in this book? Those rubrics helped you work on the areas that are most important in your writing: **Audience, Organization, Elaboration, Clarification,** and **Conventions & Skills**.

"When you take a writing test, you don't always have all the information that's on a rubric. However, you will probably have a Scoring Guide. A Scoring Guide is a lot like a rubric.

"On the next page, you can see what one student wrote in response to the writing prompt on page 226. After you read his explanation of a skill, we'll use the Scoring Guide in the writing prompt to see how well he did."

Tell Me a Story!

by Nathan Rubin

Last summer I visited the storytelling tent at the Bristol County Fair. That's where I discovered that anyone can be a terrific storyteller. It just takes a little practice.

First, you need to find a story that's worth telling. It should be funny, spooky, or surprising in some way. Maybe the story has an odd twist that teaches a lesson. Pick something your audience will remember.

It's important to tell the story in your own words. Don't try to repeat the story just the way you heard it. If you memorize a story, it won't sound fresh and interesting when you tell it.

To begin, picture the main characters. What details would make them stand out for your listeners? Think about how they move, and try to move that way when you pretend to be them in the story. For example, an old person might hunch over a little and move with a slow shuffle.

Also think about the characters' voices. Are they low and gravelly or high and squeaky? Change your voice to fit each character. Then think about sound effects that could help listeners imagine the setting. Is there a strong wind in the story? Could you make noise like traffic in the background? Can you make the sounds of animals in the story?

Next, picture the story events in the order they happen. Here's a tip to help you remember the story. Draw empty boxes in a line on a sheet of paper. If your story is long, you will need many boxes. Then draw stick figures in each box. You will show the story events in the order they take place. When you're finished, each box should show some details that you want to remember and include in your story.

Now try your story out on an audience. Choose your family or some good friends, so you won't feel nervous. Watch your audience to see how they react. Do they laugh? Do they seem surprised? Each time you tell the story, keep the parts that get the reaction you want. Then think about ways to make the other parts of your story more interesting.

When you're ready to tell your story to a real audience, relax. Take a deep breath and look around. Find a friendly face and begin telling your story to that person. Remember to make eye contact with other members of the audience as you talk. Let your listeners know that you are having fun, and they will have a good time, too.

When you're done, take a bow, and make a quick exit. It's always a good idea to leave your audience begging for more.

66 Look at each point on the Scoring Guide. Then read what Nathan wrote. See if you can find examples to show how well his explanation did on each part of the Scoring Guide. 99

Scoring Guide The writer clearly identifies the topic for the audience early in the paper.  **Audience**

66 Let's see. Right in the opening paragraph, Nathan says that anyone can be a terrific storyteller. That's his topic, the skill he's going to explain. He's going to explain how to tell stories. 99

Last summer I visited the storytelling tent at the Bristol County Fair. That's where I discovered that anyone can be a terrific storyteller. It just takes a little practice.

66 In the rest of his explanation, everything he wrote tells how to become a good storyteller. 99

Organization

The paper is well organized. The writer includes an introduction, body, and conclusion.

" Right after the introduction, Nathan starts explaining steps you can take to become a good storyteller. The body of his writing adds more details about this topic. "

First, you need to find a story that's worth telling. It should be funny, spooky, or surprising in some way. Maybe the story has an odd twist that teaches a lesson. Pick something your audience will remember.

" A good conclusion lets readers know the explanation is ending. It wraps up all the ideas. See how Nathan concludes his explanation? He tells what should happen when you finish telling a good story. "

When you're done, take a bow, and make a quick exit. It's always a good idea to leave your audience begging for more.

Elaboration

The writer includes details or facts that help readers understand each main idea.

" Nathan says to think about the characters' voices. Then he gives examples and details to help readers understand what he means. "

Also think about the characters' voices. Are they low and gravelly or high and squeaky? Change your voice to fit each character. Then think about sound effects that could help listeners imagine the setting. Is there a strong wind in the story? Could you make noise like traffic in the background? Can you make the sounds of animals in the story?

Signal words help readers follow your ideas. That's what the **clarification step** does. Can you find the signal words that Nathan included in this part of his explanation?

Next, picture the story events in the order they happen. Here's a tip to help you remember the story. Draw empty boxes in a line on a sheet of paper. If your story is long, you will need many boxes. Then draw stick figures in each box. You will show the story events in the order they take place. When you're finished, each box should show some details that you want to remember and include in your story.

The writer uses the conventions of language and spelling correctly.

Conventions & Skills

Nathan did not make any serious mistakes in capitalization, punctuation, grammar, or spelling. See?

It's important to tell the story in your own words. Don't try to repeat the story just the way you heard it. If you memorize a story, it won't sound fresh and interesting when you tell it.

Now I'm ready to write!

I will tackle a different writing prompt. You can see how well I do!

Phanna

Test Writing Champ

Name:	Phanna
Favorite Subject:	social studies
Favorite Famous Person:	Marie Curie
Hobbies:	collecting rocks, listening to country music
Assignment:	an explanation for a writing test

Prewriting

Gather

Read and analyze the writing prompt. Make sure I understand what I am supposed to do.

" Let's look at a piece of writing I am doing for a test. That will help you work on your own writing test strategies. To begin, you need to read the writing prompt carefully and find the three parts. The parts probably won't be labeled. You will need to find the setup, the task, and the **Scoring Guide** by yourself!

"Of course, the first thing writers do is gather information. When you write to take a test, you start gathering information from the writing prompt. You've got to be sure you know exactly what you're supposed to do.

"Here's the writing prompt I have. "

Setup — Where would you like to go on vacation or for a school or club trip: a historical monument, a natural wonder, a theme park, or somewhere else?

Task — (Write about the place) you would choose.
(Explain why) you want to go there. Be sure your writing

Scoring Guide
- clearly identifies the topic for your audience early in the paper.
- is well organized. You should include an introduction, body, and conclusion.
- includes details or facts that help readers understand each main idea.
- uses signal words to connect ideas.
- uses the conventions of language and spelling correctly.

> Before I do anything else, I take five minutes to study the writing prompt. I follow these steps so I know what I'm supposed to write.

1 Read all three parts of the prompt carefully.

> All right, I found the **Setup**, the **Task**, and the Scoring Guide.

2 Circle key words in the Task part of the prompt that tell what kind of writing I need to do.

> I circled the words **Write about the place**. That's my assigned topic. I also circled the words **Explain why** because that tells the kind of writing I am doing. Now I need to think of a place I want to go and the reasons why I want to go there!

3 Make sure I know how I'll be graded.

> The Scoring Guide tells what I need to include to get a good score. I will pay close attention to that!

4 Say what I need to do in my own words.

> Here's what I'm supposed to do: explain why I want to go to a particular place.

Go to page 116 in the **Practice the Strategy Notebook!**

Prewriting

Organize   Plan my time.

"Prewriting is a little different when you take a test. You need to keep an eye on the clock! Think about how much time you have and divide the time into the different parts of the writing process. If the test takes an hour, here's how I organize my time."

Analyze the prompt
5 minutes

Edit
5 minutes

Prewrite
15 minutes

Revise
10 minutes

Draft
25 minutes

Prewriting

Gather & Organize

Choose a graphic organizer. Use it to organize my ideas.

❝ I don't have much time, so I'll gather ideas and organize them at the same time. First, I'll choose a graphic organizer. I'm writing an explanation, so a network tree can help me keep track of main ideas and details. Some of the information for my network tree will come right from the Setup and Task in the writing prompt. (To review network trees, you can look in Unit 2 on page 87.) ❞

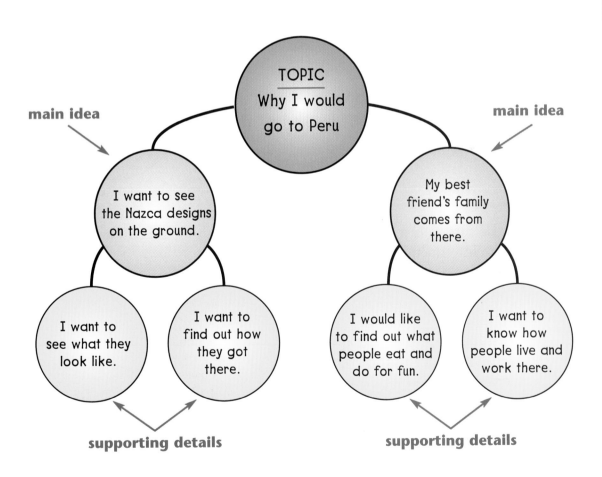

main idea

TOPIC
Why I would go to Peru

main idea

I want to see the Nazca designs on the ground.

My best friend's family comes from there.

I want to see what they look like.

I want to find out how they got there.

I would like to find out what people eat and do for fun.

I want to know how people live and work there.

supporting details

supporting details

Prewriting

Organize

Check my graphic organizer against the Scoring Guide.

> In a test, you don't always get much time to revise, so prewriting is more important than ever. Even before I write, I'll check the information on my network tree against the **Scoring Guide** in the writing prompt. My paper should do everything that's listed in the **Scoring Guide**.

Be sure your writing clearly identifies the topic for your audience early in the paper.

> I'm going to write about Peru. That's my topic, at the top of my network tree.

TOPIC
Why I would go to Peru

Be sure your writing is well organized. You should include an introduction, body, and conclusion.

> I'll use the topic to write an introduction. I'll use the main ideas from my network tree in the body.
>
> "Then I'll restate my topic in the conclusion.

I want to see the Nazca designs on the ground.

My best friend's family comes from there.

Be sure your writing includes details or facts that help readers understand each main idea.

"In the body of my writing, I'll give details about the place and my reasons for wanting to go there. The details and reasons will come from the bottom level of my network tree."

I would like to find out what people eat and do for fun.

I want to know how people live and work there.

I want to see what they look like.

I want to find out how they got there.

 Be sure your writing uses signal words to connect ideas.

"As I write, I'll remember to use signal words like **first** and **because**."

 Be sure your writing uses the conventions of language and spelling correctly.

"For my last step, I'll check for any mistakes in grammar, punctuation, capitalization, and spelling."

Go to page 117 in the **Practice** the Strategy **Notebook!**

Drafting

Write

Use my network tree to write an explanation with a good introduction, body, and conclusion.

66 After I checked my network tree one more time, here's what I wrote. I left room for corrections and tried to write neatly. 99

My Dream Trip
by Phanna

introduction

Many kids ~~like me~~ my age would go to a theme park if they could choose a trip to anywhere. Not me. I'd like to go to another country. Peru, in South America.

There are two ~~big~~ main reasons I'd like to visit Peru. My best friend's family came from there. The Nazca Lines are in Peru. Let me explain more about my reasons.

My friend Isabel has been telling me about Peru. Her family comes from an old city called cuzco. Cuzco is at such a high altitude. The sky is dark blue in the middle of the day!

body

Life is ~~kind of~~ very different there. Many people live in villages without no running water. They're homes are made of mud bricks. Although the people are poor, they like their lives. Many families have pet llamas. These animals look a little like goats with long necks. Dye the wool to make brightly colored yarn. Then they knit soft sweaters, socks, and mittens. Many tourists come to the markets to buy the villagers woolen goods.

For fun, many people play music. The flutes are maid of something like bamboo and the sound is wonderful. The music is not like nothing in the united states. Isabel said the food is ~~sorta~~ really good in Peru, too. You can get purple potatoes there!

Besides going to Peru to see how people live my other reason is to see the Nazca Lines. These ~~funny lookin~~ mysterious lines can only be seen clearly from up in a plane. Some of the designs are a few hundred feet across. Some are the shapes of different animals. Like a spider, a monkey, and a lizard.

The designs are so enormus. The lines may be 1500 to 2500 years old, so they were definitely not made by anyone who could see them from a plane. This puzzle has stumped scientists for a hundred years, since the lines were discovered. I'd really like to see the lines in person. Maybe I could be the one to figure out why they are there.

I hope to get to Peru someday. Both to see how my friend's family and other people live and to explore some mysterys of the culture. I'm sure it would be an unforgettable trip, much more then a ride in a spinning teacup.

"Remember that you may not get a chance to recopy your paper in a writing test. Try to be neat when you write."

Go to page 118 in the **Practice** the Strategy **Notebook!**

Revising

Elaborate

Check what I have written against the Scoring Guide. Add any missing facts or details.

> In a test, I can't read my paper to a partner, so I'll read it to myself. I'll keep the **Scoring Guide** in mind and see if anything is missing.
>
> "The **Scoring Guide** says that I need to include details or reasons that help readers understand each main idea. I think I should add more details about the things I'd like to see in Peru.

READ TO MYSELF

[DRAFT]

that the people who made them couldn't see the whole outline of what they made ← **added detail**

The designs are so enormus. The lines may be 1500 to 2500 years
old, so they were definitely not made by anyone who could see them
from a plane. This puzzle has stumped scientists for a hundred years,
I like collecting rocks and learning about old things, so
since the lines were discovered. I'd really like to see the lines in
person. Maybe I could be the one to figure out why they are there.

added detail

Go to page 120 in the **Practice** the Strategy **Notebook!**

Revising

Clarify

Check what I have written against the Scoring Guide. Make sure I have used signal words so that everything is clear.

READ TO MYSELF

"I'll read my paper again and check the **Scoring Guide** one more time to make sure everything is clear for my reader.

"The **Scoring Guide** says that I should use signal words to connect ideas. I think I can add some signal words that will make my ideas clearer."

[DRAFT]

signal word

First of all,
There are two ~~big~~ main reasons I'd like to visit Peru. My best
Second,
friend's family came from there. The Nazca Lines are in Peru. Let me

explain more about my reasons.

signal word
My friend Isabel has been telling me about Peru. Her family comes
Because
from an old city called cuzco. Cuzco is at such a high altitude. The

sky is dark blue in the middle of the day!

Go to page 121 in the **Practice the Strategy Notebook!**

Editing

Proofread — Check that I have used correct grammar, capitalization, punctuation, and spelling.

" The **Scoring Guide** says to use correct grammar, capitalization, punctuation, and spelling. I leave plenty of time to check for errors in these important areas.
   "We've used a checklist like the one below so often that I almost have it memorized. "

Proofreading Checklist

☑ Do the subjects and verbs agree?

☑ Have compound sentences been joined with a comma and a conjunction or with a semicolon?

☑ Have I avoided run-on sentences and fragments?

☑ Do the appropriate words begin with a capital letter?

☑ Have I formed plural nouns and possessive nouns correctly?

☑ Did I use the correct form of each pronoun?

☑ Do all pronouns have a clear antecedent? Do they agree with their antecedents?

☑ Have I avoided using double negatives?

☑ Are all words spelled correctly?

Extra Practice
See **Review** (pages CS 22–CS 23) in the back of this book.

" When I proofread my work, I found a few errors and fixed them. It's a good thing I checked my draft! "

My Dream Trip
by Phanna

[DRAFT]

Many kids ~~like me~~ my age would go to a theme park if they could choose a trip to anywhere. Not me. I'd like to go to another country, Peru, in South America.

There are two ~~big~~ main reasons I'd like to visit Peru. First of all, My best friend's family came from there. Second, The Nazca Lines are in Peru. Let me explain more about my reasons.

My friend Isabel has been telling me about Peru. Her family comes from an old city called cuzco. Because Cuzco is at such a high altitude, The sky is dark blue in the middle of the day!

Life is ~~kind of~~ very different there. Many people live in villages without ~~no~~ running water. ~~They're~~ Their homes are made of mud bricks. Although the people are poor, they like their lives. Many families have pet llamas. These animals look a little like goats with long necks. People Dye the wool to make brightly colored yarn. Then they knit soft sweaters, socks, and mittens. Many tourists come to the markets to buy the villagers' woolen goods.

For fun, many people play music. The flutes are ~~maid~~ made of something like bamboo, and the sound is wonderful. The music is not like ~~nothing~~ anything in the united states. Isabel said the food is ~~sort a~~ really good in Peru, too. You can get purple potatoes there!

that the people who made them couldn't
see the whole outline of what they made

Besides going to Peru to see how people live, my other reason is to see the Nazca Lines. These ~~funny lookin'~~ mysterious lines can only be seen clearly from up in a plane. Some of the designs are a few hundred feet across. Some are the shapes of different animals, like a spider, a monkey, and a lizard.

The designs are so enormous. The lines may be 1500 to 2500 years old, so they were definitely not made by anyone who could see them from a plane. This puzzle has stumped scientists for a hundred years, since the lines were discovered. I like collecting rocks and learning about old things, so I'd really like to see the lines in person. Maybe I could be the one to figure out why they are there.

I hope to get to Peru someday, both to see how my friend's family and other people live and to explore some mysteries of the culture. I'm sure it would be an unforgettable trip, much more than ~~then~~ a ride in a spinning teacup.

Go to page 122 in the **Practice** the Strategy **Notebook!**

We're finished! That wasn't so bad! The main thing to remember is that when you write for a test, you use the writing process. It's just a little different from other writing. Remember these important steps when you write for a test.

1. **Analyze the writing prompt before you start to write.**
   Remember, most writing prompts have three parts: the Setup, the Task, and the Scoring Guide. The parts will probably not be labeled, so you have to figure them out yourself.

2. **Make sure you understand the task before you start to write. Remember to**
   - Read all three parts of the prompt carefully.
   - Circle key words in the Task part of the prompt that tell what kind of writing you need to do. The Task might also identify your audience.
   - Make sure you know how you will be graded.
   - Describe the assignment in your own words to make sure you understand it.

3. **Keep an eye on the clock.**
   Decide how much time you are going to spend on each part of the writing process and try to stick to your schedule. Do not spend so much time on prewriting that you do not have any time left to write!

4. **Reread your writing. Check it against the Scoring Guide at least twice.**
   Remember the rubrics we have used all year? A Scoring Guide on a writing test is like a rubric. It can help you keep what is important in mind. That way, you can make sure you have done everything the Scoring Guide asks you to do.

5. **Plan, plan, plan!**
   You do not get much time to revise during a test, so planning is more important than ever.

6. **Write neatly.**
   Remember, if the people who score your test cannot read your writing, it does not matter how good your paper is!

your own **TEST** writing

Expository

Put the strategies you practiced in this unit to work. Use the idea below or come up with your own idea. Then take your own expository writing test. Pretend this is a real test and give yourself one hour to complete all of the steps.

You have been invited to suggest a person, work of art, piece of architecture, or natural wonder to be shown on a new postage stamp. Tell what you would suggest and explain the reasons for your choice. Be sure your writing

- clearly identifies the topic for your audience early in the paper.
- is well organized. You should include an introduction, body, and conclusion.
- includes details or facts that help readers understand each main idea.
- uses signal words to connect ideas.
- uses the conventions of language and spelling correctly.

portfolio

School–Home Connection

Keep a writing portfolio. Think about adding the activities from the *Practice the Strategy Notebook* to your writing portfolio. You may want to take your portfolio home to share.

Extra Practice

Conventions & SKILLS

The activities on the following pages provide additional practice in the grammar, usage, and mechanics skills you worked with throughout this book. Use the activities to get extra practice in these skills. Complete each activity on a separate sheet of paper.

Table of Contents

Forming Compound Sentences . . . . pages CS 2–CS 3

Forms of Pronouns . . . . pages CS 4–CS 5

Plural and Possessive Nouns . . . . pages CS 6–CS 7

Subject-Verb Agreement . . . . pages CS 8–CS 9

Capitalization . . . . pages CS 10–CS 11

Titles . . . . pages CS 12–CS 13

Double Negatives . . . . pages CS 14–CS 15

Direct and Indirect Quotations . . . . pages CS 16–CS 17

Pronouns and Antecedents . . . . pages CS 18–CS 19

Sentence Fragments . . . . pages CS 20–CS 21

Conventions & Skills Review . . . . pages CS 22–CS 23

 Forming Compound Sentences

When two sentences are joined together correctly, they become a **compound sentence**. When they are joined incorrectly, they become a **run-on**.

ReView the Rule

- Compound sentences can be formed by placing a **comma** and a **coordinating conjunction** between two related sentences. The words *and, but,* and *or* are coordinating conjunctions.

    Run-on: Swimming is fun but it can be dangerous.
    Correct: Swimming is fun, but it can be dangerous.

- Compound sentences can also be formed by placing a **semicolon** (;) between two related sentences.

    Run-on: Everyone should learn how to swim this skill can save a life.
    Correct: Everyone should learn how to swim; this skill can save a life.

Practice

Correct each run-on below by rewriting it as a compound sentence. Number a separate sheet of paper 1.–15. You can choose whether to join the sentences with a comma and a conjunction or with a semicolon.

1. You should always swim with a friend it is dangerous to swim alone.

2. It is fun to swim in the sunshine but the sun can burn your skin.

3. Sunscreen protects your skin but you must apply it often.

4. There are often numbers on the side of a swimming pool they show the depth of the water.

5. You can swim in the shallow end but you should never dive into shallow water.

6. The deep end of a pool can be dangerous only good swimmers should go there.

7. Many beaches and pools have lifeguards they are ready to help in emergencies.

8. Lifeguards must earn lifesaving certificates and they must also have first-aid certificates.

9. Lifeguards must be alert they save many lives each year.

10. Most pools and beaches have rules and swimmers must obey the rules at all times.

11. You should never push someone into the water and you should always watch out for other swimmers.

12. You must be careful on a water slide or you might hurt yourself or another swimmer.

13. You must not swim near the diving boards or someone might land on top of you.

14. Diving can be fun but you must learn how to dive safely.

15. Always wait quietly for your turn on the diving board divers need to concentrate.

On another sheet of paper, rewrite this paragraph, correcting any compound sentences that have been formed incorrectly.

I love to go to the pool with my friends but I don't know how to swim. My mother tried to teach me my uncle tried, too. Some people were just not meant to be fish you can enjoy the water without swimming in it. I am going to scout camp next week. Maybe I will learn to swim there but please don't count on it!

Forms of Pronouns

Pronouns are words that take the place of nouns.

ReView the Rule

1. The **subject pronouns** are *I, he, she, we,* and *they.* Subject pronouns are used when the pronoun is the subject of a sentence.

2. The **object pronouns** are *me, him, her, us,* and *them.* Object pronouns are used when the pronoun is a direct object or the object of a preposition.

3. The words **you** and **it** can be used as subject and object pronouns.

4. **Possessive pronouns,** including *my, your, his, her, its,* and *their,* show ownership.

5. When you write about yourself and another person, always name the other person first.

> **Incorrect:** I and Kim are in the same group.
> **Correct:** Kim and I are in the same group.

Practice

Number your paper from 1.–15. Choose the correct form of each pronoun and write it on your paper. Then write the number of the rule above that applies.

1. When (I and my family/my family and I/my family and me) went to Alaska, we got to see the northern lights.

2. A French scientist named Pierre Gassendi saw the northern lights in 1621; (he/him/his) named (they/them/their) the aurora borealis.

3. Aurora was a character from Roman mythology; (she/her) was the goddess of the dawn.

4. Boreas was also a character from mythology; the Romans called (he/him) the god of the north wind.

5. The lights begin late at night, and (they/them) continue until dawn.

6. Sometimes the northern lights were very bright; (my brother and me/me and my brother/my brother and I) could read without any other light.

7. (I and my dad/My dad and I/Me and my dad) looked up the best viewing times.

8. If strong moonlight hits (they/them), the lights look blue.

9. (My family and I/I and my family/My family and me) drove far away from the city to see the northern lights.

10. Another tourist told (me and my brother/my brother and me/my brother and I) that near midnight is the best viewing time.

11. When people first saw these lights long ago, (they/them) could not figure out what was happening.

12. An Alaskan girl told (me and Mom/Mom and me/Mom and I) that she never whistles at the northern lights.

13. According to a legend, whistling makes the lights come close to people and snatch (them/they) away.

14. When (my brother and I/me and my brother/my brother and me) saw the aurora borealis, we took many pictures.

15. Watching the aurora borealis always makes (my mom and me/me and my mom/my mom and I) happy.

Read this part of a draft about the northern lights. On your paper, rewrite the paragraph, correcting the pronoun errors. Underline the correct pronouns. You should find and correct seven errors.

Him and I stood quietly watching the northern lights. Them hypnotized we. At times, it seemed as if us could reach out and touch they. We knew that wasn't possible, though. A glowing arc suddenly appeared in front of me and him. The arc stretched high into the sky, and then it disappeared from us sight. We stared into the night, wondering what would happen next.

A **plural noun** names more than one person, place, or thing. Regular plural nouns are formed by adding **-s** and **-es**. Irregular plural nouns have many different spellings. A **possessive noun** shows ownership. Plural nouns and possessive nouns are sometimes confused because both often end in **s**.

ReView the Rule

Plural Nouns

- Add *-s* or *-es* to form the plural of most nouns.

   Examples: building ⟶ building**s**; bench ⟶ bench**es**

- Change *y* to *i* and add *-es* to form the plural of some nouns ending in *y*.

   Example: story ⟶ stor**ies**

- Change *f* to *v* and add *-es* to form the plural of some nouns ending in *f*.

   Example: wife ⟶ wi**ves**

- Some nouns change their spelling or remain unchanged in their plural form.

   Examples: goose ⟶ geese; deer ⟶ deer

Possessive Nouns

- Add an **apostrophe** and *-s* to form the possessive of singular and plural nouns that do not end in *s*.

   Examples: the woman**'s** car; the women**'s** cars

- Add only an apostrophe to form the possessive of plural nouns **that** end in *s*.

   Example: the Mohawks**'** traditions

Let's practice the rules for forming plural and possessive nouns. On your paper, number 1.–15. Then find the error in each sentence below and write the correct plural or possessive noun form. Label it **PL** for plural or **POSS** for possessive.

1. Zookeepers care for animals at zoos, especially the babys.

2. Most peoples become zookeepers because they love animals.

3. They take time to answer childrens questions.

4. They tell the children not to give candys to the animals.

5. Zookeepers may care for everything from sheeps to sharks.

6. They must know what leafs and other foods each animal eats.

7. Some animals eat tomatos and other vegetables.

8. Other animals, such as wolfs, eat only meat.

9. Zookeepers have a powerful influence on the animals lives.

10. They must know when an animal needs a veterinarians help.

11. Veterinarians are sometimes heros at the zoo.

12. They protect animals from many varietys of disease.

13. They can diagnose an illness just by looking at an animals eyes.

14. A zookeepers life is a busy one.

15. Many zoos success depends on the keepers' skill.

Apply

On your paper, rewrite this part of a descriptive essay. Correct four mistakes in plural and possessive nouns. Underline the nouns you have corrected, and label them **PL** for plural or **POSS** for possessive.

Crystal is currently working in the zoos nursery. She takes care of orphaned baby gorillas and treats them like childs. The little gorilla's often rush to sit in Crystals lap.

Subject-Verb Agreement

Singular subjects take **singular verbs**. **Plural subjects** take **plural verbs**. If you learn the following rules, you will always know how to make subjects and verbs agree.

ReView the Rule

- **Verbs With Singular Subjects**

    Add **-s** or **-es** to a verb when the subject is singular.

    Examples: A carnivorous **plant eats** animals.

    It needs the animal's nitrogen.

- **Verbs With Plural Subjects**

    Do not add **-s** or **-es** when the subject is a plural noun or is one of the pronouns *I, you, we,* or *they.*

    Examples: **Venus flytraps** grow in bogs.

    They trap insects.

- **Using Forms of the Verb "to be"**

    Use *am* after *I.*
    Example: **I am** interested in carnivorous plants.

    Use *is* or *was* after singular subjects.
    Example: My Venus flytrap **plant is** very healthy.

    Use *are* or *were* with plural subjects.
    Example: Carnivorous **plants are** rare.

Practice

Number your paper 1.–15. Write the subject and verb in each sentence. If they do not agree, write the whole sentence, correcting the error.

1. Venus flytraps grow in the bogs of North and South Carolina.
2. They sprout in very wet ground.
3. They eats flies, bees, and ants.
4. The Venus flytrap leaf lies on the ground.
5. A bright red color on the leaf attract insects.
6. A sweet liquid is on the edge of the leaf.
7. This sweet liquid also lure insects onto the leaf.
8. Then the two sections of the leaf snaps together quickly.
9. Only small insects escapes between the sharp points.
10. After a while, the leaf closes tightly.
11. The Venus flytrap surround the body with liquid.
12. The decomposing insect give the plant its nitrogen.
13. Bees pollinate the flowers safely.
14. I put my finger inside a Venus flytrap.
15. It were actually painless.

Apply

In this paragraph, some of the subjects and verbs do not agree. Rewrite the paragraph on your paper, correcting the errors.

> Two flies darts around the Venus flytrap. Finally one comes to the edge of the leaf and lick the sweet-smelling liquid. It steps farther onto the leaf. Suddenly, the plant snap shut! The fly struggles. The trap tightens, and the fly disappear.

Capitalization

Proper nouns name a particular person, place, or thing. They are also used to form proper adjectives. Proper nouns can include initials, and they can be used in abbreviations. The first letter in all of these forms of proper nouns should be capitalized.

ReView the Rule

1. Capitalize the first letter in proper nouns:
   Missouri **R**iver, **S**acajawea

2. Capitalize the first letter in proper adjectives:
   Native **A**merican legend, **S**hoshoni chief

3. Capitalize the initials in proper nouns:
   Ben **N**. **C**ampbell, **W.C**. **W**yeth

4. Capitalize abbreviations of words that are capitalized when written out: **U.S**. (**U**nited **S**tates), **N.D**. (**N**orth **D**akota)

Practice

Let's put the rules for capitalization to work. Number your paper 1.–15. Find words and abbreviations in each sentence that have errors in capitalization. Write them correctly. Also write the number of the rule you applied.

1. The story of Sacajawea has become an american folk legend.

2. sacajawea means "bird woman" in the Shoshoni language.

3. Sacajawea was born in the 1780s, and her father was a shoshoni chief.

4. She grew up in the area of the United States that became montana and utah.

5. Sacajawea's husband was a french-Canadian fur trader named Toussaint Charbonneau.

6. Meriwether Lewis and william clark hired Charbonneau as an interpreter.

7. Lewis and Clark let charbonneau bring Sacajawea with him.

8. The expedition traveled through Shoshoni territory in the rocky mountains.

9. The american explorers stopped in the village where Sacajawea had been born.

10. The Villagers wanted to kill the explorers.

11. Sacajawea helped save the Explorers' lives.

12. Lewis and Clark reached the Pacific Ocean in november of 1805.

13. W. c. Wyeth painted a famous picture of Sacajawea guiding Lewis and Clark.

14. The united states congress decided to issue a coin honoring Sacajawea.

15. The new u.s. dollar has her image on it.

Read this paragraph from a research report about Sacajawea. Rewrite the paragraph on your paper, correcting all errors in capitalization.

Although a stone on the wind river reservation marks the grave of sacajawea, no one really knows when or how she died. One legend says that sacajawea died in 1812 when she was only 25 years old. Other legends tell of a shoshoni woman who lived to be 100 years old and died at fort washakie in wyoming. This woman claimed to be sacajawea and knew many details about the u.s. expedition led by meriwether lewis and william clark.

Titles are the names of books, movies, poems, songs, stories, and television series and episodes.

ReView the Rule

1. For all titles, capitalize the first word, last word, and all other words except articles, short prepositions, and conjunctions.

2. Underline or italicize the titles of books, movies, and television series.

3. Use quotation marks around titles of songs, stories, poems, and television episodes.

Practice

Now let's use what you have learned. Number your paper 1.–15. Rewrite each incorrect title correctly. Add the number of the rule above that applies. If the title in the sentence is correct, write **Correct**.

1. When you were younger, you probably watched <u>sesame street</u> on television.

2. Did you know that Sesame Street has won more Emmy awards than any other children's program?

3. Young children love to sing Elmo's Song.

4. Older children are more likely to watch shows such as Bill Nye, the science Guy and Nick News.

5. Many people watch reruns of <u>The Addams Family and the munsters.</u>

6. The Munsters was first shown on TV in 1964.

7. The first episode was titled My Fair Munster.

8. Maybe you enjoy <u>National Geographic Special</u> and other programs that take you around the world.

9. National geographic special has been nominated for Emmy awards nearly 100 times.

10. My favorite episode was called Air Force One.

11. My brother has watched an episode called Leopards of Zanzibar three times.

12. National Geographic also contributed to the movie pearl harbor.

13. <u>ABC's Wide World of Sports</u> has won more awards than any other sports show.

14. In 2001, wide world of sports celebrated its fortieth anniversary.

15. Wide World of Sports also publishes books, such as Race Across America.

Read this paragraph about television's Emmy Awards. Rewrite the paragraph on your paper, correcting the errors in capitalization, underlining, and punctuation.

> The Emmy Awards go to actors, writers, and others who work in television. Each year, TV series such as The west wing and frasier are nominated as best shows in different categories. Will any series ever catch up to "The Mary Tyler Moore Show"? It won 29 Emmy Awards.

Conventions & Skills — Double Negatives

Negatives include words such as *no, not, none, nothing, nobody, no one, nowhere, hardly, barely, neither,* and *never.*

ReView the Rule

Use only one **negative** in a sentence. If you use two of these words in a sentence, you are using a **double negative,** which is a grammar error.

Incorrect: There **wasn't no** one on the playground.

Correct: There was **no** one on the playground.
There **wasn't** anyone on the playground.

Practice

Now let's practice avoiding double negatives. Number your paper 1.–15. Read each sentence. If it is correct, write **Correct** on your paper. If the sentence contains a double negative, rewrite the sentence correctly. Remember that you often can correct a double negative in more than one way.

1. Everyone has read fables, which usually feature talking animals.

2. Some readers have not never heard of Aesop.

3. Historians do not know nothing about his life.

4. Most experts believe that he was not a real person.

5. Aesop's fables are not hardly the only popular fables.

6. Another famous writer of fables was the French author Jean de La Fontaine.

7. La Fontaine first followed the pattern set by Aesop, but later he focused on political topics.

8. Many lovers of fables believe that La Fontaine cannot be surpassed by no one as a storyteller.

9. Nobody can't forget his clever story of <u>The Fox and the Crow</u>.

10. No one can leave Lewis Carroll out when listing modern fable writers.

11. To many readers, his story <u>Alice in Wonderland</u> doesn't have no equals.

12. Fable fans must not forget Joel Chandler Harris or Beatrix Potter neither.

13. Joel Chandler Harris wrote the Bre'r Rabbit tales, fables set in the American South.

14. Some readers feel that there has not never been a better fable than Beatrix Potter's <u>Peter Rabbit</u>.

15. J.R.R. Tolkien's <u>Hobbit</u> is a fable, but his imaginary creatures are not no real animals.

Some sentences in this fable contain double negatives. Rewrite the fable to correct the errors.

A peacock went to Juno, the queen of the gods. "There isn't nothing I would like better than to have a pretty singing voice like the other birds," he explained.

Juno replied, "You're not no good singer, but you do have a beautiful tail."

"But what about my ugly voice?" the peacock said.

Juno frowned. "Go away and don't never complain no more. If I gave you a beautiful voice, you would just find some other reason to be unhappy!"

Direct and Indirect Quotations

A **direct quotation** is a speaker's exact words. An **indirect quotation** retells a speaker's words.

ReView the Rule

For a **direct quotation**, use quotation marks at the beginning and end of the speaker's exact words. Use a comma to separate the speaker's exact words from the rest of the sentence. Begin a direct quotation with a capital letter and add end punctuation before the last quotation mark.

Example: Cora said, "I think mysteries are both fun and interesting."

An **indirect quotation** is not placed in quotation marks. It often begins with the word *that* or *whether*.

Example: Cora said that she thinks mysteries are both fun and interesting.

Practice

Now let's practice what you've learned about direct and indirect quotations. Number your paper 1.–15. Read each sentence. If the sentence is a direct quotation, write **D** on your paper. Then rewrite the sentence as an *indirect* quotation. If the sentence is an indirect quotation, write **I** on your paper. Then rewrite the sentence as a *direct* quotation.

1. Professor Holman announced to us that her talk would be about the history of mystery stories.

2. "Many readers consider Edgar Allan Poe to be the inventor of the modern mystery story," she said.

3. The professor explained that Poe's mysteries thrilled readers.

4. "Another early detective novel was *The Moonstone* by Wilkie Collins," she continued.

5. She added, "Collins was a good friend of Charles Dickens, another famous novelist."

6. I whispered to my mother that I had read a story by Wilkie Collins.

7. The professor said, "In 1887, the world's most famous literary detective appeared."

8. She explained that the detective was Sherlock Holmes.

9. She added that Holmes became an instant hit with readers.

10. "Is there anyone who does not recognize the tall, thin detective with the pipe and famous hat?" she asked.

11. "The Sherlock Holmes stories are told by his friend, Dr. Watson," she continued.

12. She added that *The Hound of the Baskervilles* is her favorite Holmes tale.

13. "Another interesting English detective was Father Brown," said the professor.

14. Then she asked whether the audience had a favorite Agatha Christie character.

15. "This English author is the creator of Miss Marple," she said.

This section of a mystery contains both direct and indirect quotations. Rewrite it on your paper, correcting the punctuation errors.

> As they entered the creepy old house, Robert and Jenny held their breath. Robert told Jenny that "he hoped the staircase was strong enough to hold them".
>
> "I hope so, too. Jenny replied in a whisper.
>
> As he put his hand on the stair railing, Robert heard "a strange, moaning sound."
>
> There's something behind that door! "Jenny screamed."

Pronouns and Antecedents

A **pronoun** is a word that replaces a noun. An **antecedent** is the word or phrase that a pronoun replaces. The antecedent of each pronoun should be clear. Pronouns must also agree with their antecedents in number.

Review the Rule

- The **antecedent** of a pronoun should be clear.

  Unclear: She checked the books and the reviews and is pleased with **them**. (Does *them* refer to books or reviews?)

  Clear: She checked the book reviews and is pleased with **them**. (The antecedent of *them* has to be *reviews*.)

- A **singular antecedent** requires a **singular pronoun**.

  Incorrect: A good **reviewer** tries to give the pros and cons of the novel **they** choose. (*Reviewer* is singular, but *they* is plural.)

  Correct: A good **reviewer** tries to give the pros and cons of the novel **she** chooses. (*Reviewer* and *she* are both singular.)

- A **plural antecedent** requires a **plural pronoun**.

  Incorrect: The book **reviewers** selected **his** book carefully. (*Reviewers* is plural, but *his* is singular.)

  Correct: The book **reviewers** selected **their** books carefully. (*Reviewers* and *their* are both plural.)

Practice

Number a separate sheet of paper 1.–10. If the pronoun and its antecedent agree, write them both. If the pronoun and its antecedent do not agree, write the whole sentence, correcting the error.

1. Quakers are a small group of people, but they have had a strong influence on world history.

2. Quakers consider George Fox to be the founder of her religion, the Society of Friends.

3. Early Quakers faced many challenges. Most English people were suspicious of him.

4. The Quakers refused to remove their hats when an important person passed.

5. Friends also used the words *thee* and *thou* instead of *you*. Some of them still use these words today.

6. Early Quakers also dressed in plain, simple clothes. They were mostly black or gray.

7. A Quaker today does not wear unusual clothes. Many of them, however, try to live a simple life.

8. Friends have helped people around the world for many years. For example, it has helped war refugees.

9. Quakers believe that they have a special mission to work for peace.

10. Some people confuse Quakers with Amish people. He is very different, however.

In this paragraph from a book review, two pronouns and their antecedents do not agree in number. Another antecedent is unclear. Rewrite the paragraph on your paper, correcting the errors.

In this book, Sheila Penrose describes groups such as the Mohawk, Seneca, and Abenaki. It used to live in the Northeast. She also includes beautiful color illustrations of clothing, homes, and artwork. It is breathtaking, with many fine details. Any reader interested in Native Americans should make this book their first choice!

Sentence Fragments

A **sentence fragment** is a group of words that is punctuated like a sentence but is missing either a subject or a verb.

Review the Rule

A **complete sentence** has both a subject and a verb and expresses a complete thought. If a group of words is punctuated like a sentence but lacks either a subject or a verb, it is a **sentence fragment**.

Examples:

Sentence Fragment: Shelters in many communities throughout the state. (a subject without a verb)

Sentence Fragment: Are working hard to come up with new ideas. (a verb without a subject)

Complete Sentence: Many **experts have** ideas for solving the problem of stray animals. (a complete sentence with both a subject and a verb)

Practice

Number a separate sheet of paper 1.–15. Read the sentences below. If a sentence is complete, write **Correct**. If the words are a sentence fragment, rewrite the sentence and correct the error. Write **S** if you added a subject or **V** if you added a verb.

1. The Humane Society of the United States is the world's largest animal protection organization.

2. Has millions of supporters around the country.

3. Was founded in 1954.

4. Its staff includes veterinarians, scientists, and lawyers.

5. The Society's focus on companion animals, such as dogs and cats.

6. The Humane Society is also concerned with farm, circus, and zoo animals.

7. Pet overpopulation, a serious nationwide problem.

8. In 27 states, pets adopted from shelters must be spayed or neutered.

9. Helps to prevent pet overpopulation.

10. Helps to train animal shelter workers.

11. Work with police and judges to prevent animal abuse.

12. Opposes cruel methods of hunting and trapping.

13. Humane Society International is a worldwide organization.

14. Also supports a youth education division.

15. The group's encouragement of respect for and kindness toward animals.

Here is the body of a short letter to the director of an animal shelter. Rewrite it, adding the missing parts of a business letter. Make up information, if necessary. Also, correct any sentence fragments you find.

Our class would like to visit your shelter. We would like to know when would be a good time. Don't want to get in the way. One teacher, one parent, and about 23 students. We are eager to see the animals and find out how we can help. Please reply by February 4, if possible.

Proofreading Checklist

☑ Do the subjects and verbs agree?

☑ Have compound sentences been joined with a comma and a conjunction or with a semicolon?

☑ Have I avoided run-on sentences and fragments?

☑ Do the appropriate words begin with a capital letter?

☑ Have I formed plural nouns and possessive nouns correctly?

☑ Did I use the correct form of each pronoun?

☑ Do all pronouns have a clear antecedent? Do they agree with their antecedents?

☑ Have I avoided using double negatives?

☑ Are all words spelled correctly?

Practice

Number a sheet of paper 1.–20. Rewrite each sentence, correcting any errors in grammar, capitalization, punctuation, or spelling. Use the checklist to help you.

1. Our class take a trip to a historic place every year.

2. Last year the class voted to visit boston, massachusetts.

3. The Freedom trail is a great way to see everything and it is free.

4. The trail through the streets begin on the Boston Common.

5. The place where British soldiers drilled.

6. As we past the graves of Samuel adams and John Hancock, I remembered reading about him.

7. Next we visited a bilding called the old south meeting house.

8. The famous Boston Tea Party began their.

9. The trail then took us to Paul Reveres house.

10. It was completed in 1677, it's the oldest house in Boston.

11. The Old North church with its steeple were just a few blocks away.

12. This is where two lantern's warned that the british were coming.

13. Our guide took a picture of Katrina and I.

14. What is that Monument on the hill!

15. It honors the heros of the Battle of Bunker hill.

16. The USS *Constitution* is docked in Boston Harbor but it is usually called "Old Ironsides."

17. The ship was closed for the day we were not able to see nothing.

18. We rested on benches that were put there for tourists' to use.

19. Near the Boston common were another well-know memorial.

20. It honors the african american soldiers who fought in the Civil War.

Copy the following travel brochure on your paper. Correct any mistakes.

Visit New England Now!

- Fall is the best time to see vermont.
- The summers noisy crouds have all gone home.
- Trees are turning colors and the air is cool and fresh.
- Everyones favorite time of year.
- Give we a chance to show you a good time.

Writer's HandBook

The Writer's Handbook is designed to give you more help as well as some great hints for making your writing the best it can be. It uses the Gather, Organize, Write, Elaborate, Clarify, Proofread, and Share categories you have become familiar with during the course of this book. Use the Writer's Handbook any time you have more questions or just need a little extra help.

Table of Contents

Prewriting/Gather
Research . . . . HB 2
Getting Ideas for Writing . . HB 6

Prewriting/Organize
Note Taking . . . . HB 13
Graphic Organizers . . . . . . HB 14
Outlining . . . . HB 14

Drafting/Write
Writing Paragraphs . . . . . . HB 16
Writing a Five-Paragraph Essay HB 20
Writing Poetry . . . . HB 24

Revising/Elaborate and Clarify
Thesaurus . . . . HB 27
Dictionary . . . . HB 28
Web Sites . . . . HB 28

Editing/Proofread
Capitalization . . . . HB 29
Sentence Structure . . . . . . HB 29

Simple, Compound, and
Complex Sentences . . . . . . HB 31
Subject-Verb Agreement . . . HB 32
Abbreviations . . . . HB 33
Quotation Marks . . . . HB 34
End Marks . . . . HB 34
Commas . . . . HB 35
Parts of Speech . . . . HB 35
Negatives . . . . HB 40
Homophones . . . . HB 40
Signal Words . . . . HB 41
Writing a Letter . . . . HB 42
Addressing Letters . . . . . . HB 42

Publishing/Share
Ways to Publish . . . . HB 43

**Listening, Speaking,
and Thinking Skills** . . . . HB 44

Research

Research is an important part of writing. When you look for information about a topic, you are doing research. It's important to use good sources.

A **source** is anything or anyone with information. **Primary sources** include books or people that are closest to the information. Diaries, journals, and other writings of people who lived during the described events are considered primary sources. **Secondary sources** are books or people who use other books or people to get information. Primary and secondary sources fit into three categories—**printed, electronic,** and **personal**.

Use a variety of primary and secondary sources from different categories when you do research. That way you can make sure the information is accurate and you will have lots of it to choose from. Talk to your teacher about how many sources and what kinds of sources to use for different writing projects.

- **Printed sources** include books, magazines, newspapers, letters, journals and diaries, and reference materials such as encyclopedias and dictionaries.

- **Electronic sources** include the Internet, television, radio, and videos.

- **Personal sources** include people you interview or observe and your own experiences and memories.

When doing research, keep these points in mind:

- When you use sources, be sure they are **credible** ones. Credible means that the source can be trusted to have accurate information. Generally, books, magazines, and reference materials can be considered credible sources. People who are experts in their field and those you know and trust personally are also credible sources.

- Use caution when using Web sites, movies, and television as sources. Many Web sites offer the opinion of the people who created them, not necessarily the facts about a topic. Check several Web sites and some printed sources on the same topic to be sure you are getting "just the facts." Also, Web sites often move or become outdated, so check to see that the ones you are using are still in operation. Finally, make sure you have an adult—a teacher or parent—help you as you do research on the Internet.

- Movies and television offer a lot of information, but it is often difficult to tell if the information is fact, fiction, or someone's opinion. Again, double check with other sources and with an adult to be sure you are getting accurate information.

Printed

Sources	Books, Magazines, Newspapers, Reference Materials, Letters, Journals/Diaries
Where to Find Them	Library, Home, School, Bookstores, Discount Department Stores
How to Use Them	Use headings to find useful information. Read. Take notes while reading.
How to Cite Them (Use punctuation and capitalization as shown.)	**Books:** Author's Last Name, First Name. <u>Book Title</u>. City: Publishing Company, year. **Magazine Articles:** Author's Last Name, First Name. "Title of Article." <u>Title of Magazine</u>, volume number (if there is one), date, month, or season, and year of publication: page number. (If the article is longer than one page, state the first page and the last page of the article with a dash between them.) **Encyclopedias/Dictionaries:** Title of Encyclopedia or Dictionary, edition number (ed. __), s.v. "item." (If you looked up Olympic Games, it would be s.v. "Olympic Games.") **Letters/Diaries/Journals:** Mention them in the text as you are writing, rather than citing them later.

Electronic

The Internet,
Television,
Radio,
Videos

The Internet,
Television,
Radio,
Stores, Library

Read Web sites.
Watch the news on television.
Listen to radio programs.
Rent or check out videos.
Take notes as you are reading,
watching, and listening.

Internet: State the Web address of
the Web sites you used. Most Web
addresses will begin with http://
and end with .com, .net, .org, or
.edu.

Films/Videos: Title of Film or Video.
City where the production company
is located: Production Company
Name, year.

Television/Radio: Mention them in
the text as you are writing, rather
than citing them later.

Personal

Self,
Other People

Home: Parents, Siblings,
Grandparents
School: Teachers, Principals,
Librarians, Friends, Other Family
Members, People in the Community

Listen to people when they tell stories.
Interview people who know something
about your topic.
Ask questions.
Take notes.

Personal sources should be
mentioned in the text as you are
writing.
When interviewing, you can quote
the person by enclosing his or her
exact words in quotation marks. You
can also use phrases such as "according to" to give credit to your source.
To give credit to personal sources
other than people you interview,
simply state where you found the
information.

Getting Ideas for Writing

So you have a writing assignment. Now what? Where do you begin? Your mind might be a complete blank right now. You haven't even chosen a topic yet. The early stages of writing are the toughest ones. Good writers use all kinds of techniques to generate new ideas. Here are some ideas to help you get started.

Brainstorming

Brainstorming is a great way to generate lots of ideas in a short amount of time. You can brainstorm alone or with a group of people. All you have to do is say or think one word, and you're off! Here's how it works:

Your assignment is to write an expository essay about an animal. If you're working in a group, the members of the group can brainstorm together. One person starts by saying "animals." The rest of the group can now take turns saying words or phrases that come to mind. Someone says "mammals." Someone else says "reptiles." Another person says "dinosaurs." As this is happening, members of the group should be careful to take turns and give each other time to write down what's being said. As the process continues, you or someone else in the group will probably say something that will become the topic for your essay.

If you're working alone, the process is the same. Think of the initial assignment. Write down words related to the assignment as they come to mind. Eventually, you will find the one word or phrase that will become the topic for your essay. Remember to write down your thoughts as you brainstorm alone, too. That way, if you change your mind, you'll have other choices to work with.

A journal is similar to a diary. Both
are used to write down personal
thoughts. However, diaries are usually
used to record daily events and
Journals are generally used
oughts, impressions, and
A journal is a

Journaling

A journal is similar to a diary. Both are used to write down personal thoughts. However, diaries are usually used to record daily events and feelings. Journals are generally used to record thoughts, impressions, and responses to events. A journal is a great way to generate ideas for writing.

Writers who use journals keep one with them most of the time. You might want to keep your journal in your book bag or locker and take it home with you after school. That way, when an interesting thought occurs to you, you can write it in your journal no matter where you are. The great thing about journaling is that there's no right or wrong way to do it. It's also great because you don't have to try to keep every good idea in your head. Just write it down and it will always be there, ready to become a topic for writing.

Freewriting

Freewriting is a very unusual method of writing because it has no form. The idea behind freewriting is to write down everything that comes to mind during a specific period of time. Just get out a piece of paper and a pen or pencil, or sit down in front of a computer. For the next few minutes, jot down everything your mind comes up with, even stuff that doesn't make any sense. You don't have to use complete sentences. You don't have to worry about spelling. You don't even have to write words. You can draw, sketch, or doodle as part of freewriting.

When time is up, stop writing (or doodling) and look at what you've got. Read it over a couple of times. You'll be amazed at what you might find. Some of the best ideas for writing show up in the middle of freewriting.

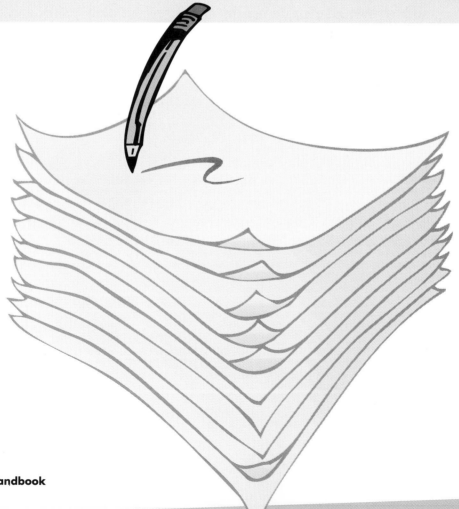

Daydreaming

This one is best done at home. Your teachers probably won't appreciate your daydreaming during class, and daydreaming while crossing the road is downright dangerous.

Try this. When you have some free time at home, get a mug of something good to drink (hot chocolate works great on a cold day). Now find a comfortable spot and—are you ready for this?—don't do anything! At least, don't do anything specific. Daydreaming means letting your mind wander wherever it wants to go. Stare out the window. Watch the goldfish in your fish tank. Listen to the rain. Smell dinner cooking in the kitchen. Think about what you'll be when you're an adult. Something will probably come to mind that will make a great topic for writing.

Here's a tip for how to use daydreaming. As soon as you hit upon a great topic for writing, get up and write down everything you can think of before you forget it. You can organize it later, but it's very important to record it all now. Just like dreams you dream at night, daydreams will disappear quickly, and you don't want to lose all those great ideas.

Reading

Sometimes the easiest way to get ideas for writing is to read. For example, let's say you have been asked to write a piece of narrative historical fiction. You don't know much about history. How do you write about something you don't know? Make use of your library.

Talk to your school librarian or go to the public library and ask for help at the information desk. These people are experts. Tell them you are looking for a few books about history. They will probably ask you some questions such as, "What kind of history are you interested in reading about?" or, "Would you like books about U.S. history or world history?" These questions will help you to make some early decisions about your writing. Once you decide what kind of history you want to read about, pick a few books that are short enough to read quickly, but long enough to have lots of interesting information. Again, people who work at libraries can help you through this process.

As you read about history, you will spot things that interest you. Write down those things. Skip over the stuff you don't find interesting, at least for now. When you are finished reading, look at the notes you took. Do they have anything in common? Do most of them have something to do with specific time periods, people, or things in history? For example, in reading about U.S. history, did you always stop at the sections about inventions because you found that information interesting? Maybe you can focus your writing assignment on an invention or an inventor.

Don't forget to read for your own interest and pleasure. The more you read, the more you'll know. The more you know, the more ideas for writing you will have.

TV/Movies

Great ideas for writing may be as close as your television or movie theater. There are cable channels that run programs specifically about science, technology, history, animals, cooking, music, sports, and just about any other topic you can think of. Public television also has great documentaries and programs about interesting and unusual topics.

Movies can also be good for generating ideas for writing—especially movies that deal with specific topics. Are you a fan of sci-fi movies? You can use your favorite sci-fi movie to come up with ideas for an expository essay about artificial intelligence or a compare-and-contrast report about robots and computers.

Just as you should use caution when using television and movies as sources when you write, be cautious in using them to generate ideas. Make sure you talk to an adult about appropriate and safe choices in movies and television programs.

Interviewing

An interview is the process of asking questions of another person and listening to and recording that person's answers. Interviews make good sources for writing projects, especially if the person you interview is an expert about your topic. Interviews can also be good ways to generate ideas for writing.

Some of the most interesting stories come from people in your community and family. Your parents and grandparents have lived through many events. Sit down with a family member or another trusted adult and ask that person to tell you about a memorable event he or she experienced or an interesting person he or she knew. You'll be amazed at the stories you will hear. Many famous authors say that their stories were inspired by what other people have told them.

As you listen to people's stories, jot down notes. It's safe to say that something the person said during the interview will probably give you a good idea for your own writing project.

Prewriting
Organize

Note Taking

As you are doing research for your writing project, you will want to take notes. That way you will have the most important information in small pieces that you can use easily. However, taking notes can be tricky, especially for the beginner. Here are some things to keep in mind:

- Keep your notes short. You don't have to use complete sentences, as long as you include the important information.

- Make sure your handwriting is legible. If you scribble, you may not be able to read your own notes later.

- Use note cards. That way you can arrange your notes without having to rewrite them. Try using different colors of note cards to help you organize your notes.

- When listening to a speaker and taking notes, don't try to write down what the speaker is saying "word for word." Just make sure you get the important stuff.

- When you are interviewing, however, you will want to get the exact words down on paper. In this case, ask the speaker to repeat what he or she said, so you can write the quote. If it's possible, use a tape recorder during the interview, so you can listen to the quote as often as you need to. Just make sure you get the speaker's permission to record the interview.

- It's important to write down the source of your information on your note cards as you are taking notes. That way you can cite or credit your sources easily.

Graphic Organizers

A graphic organizer is a tool that helps writers put information in order before they start a draft. Graphic organizers include storyboards, sequence chains, spider maps, network trees, support patterns, attribute charts, cause-and-effect chains, story maps, pros-and-cons charts, 5 W's charts, order-of-importance organizers, main idea tables, Venn diagrams, and outlines. When you do other writing projects, you'll want to continue to use them to help you keep track of information. What kind of graphic organizers you use depends on what kind of writing project you have. Check back with this book to see what kind of graphic organizer works best for different writing projects.

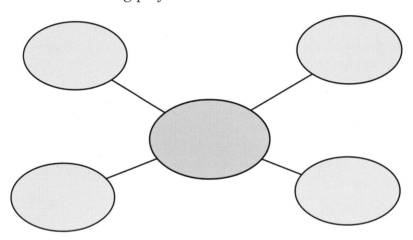

Outlining

There are many ways to organize information. One very useful organizer that you have used is an outline. The outline helps you put your information in the order it will appear in your writing. The outline can be divided into several basic pieces—the introduction, the body, and the conclusion—just like a basic essay. Every letter and number in the outline stands for something in your essay. Words or phrases that are designated with Roman numerals represent entire chunks of an essay. Words or phrases that are designated with capital letters represent paragraphs which support a main statement or idea. Words or phrases that are designated with regular numbers represent specific details. Here's a basic outline.

I. Introduction

gets audience's attention ——→ **A. Lead**

moves closer to the main idea ——→ **B. Related statement**

states main idea of essay ——→ **C. Transitional statement**

introduce the essay to the audience

II. Body

states main idea of paragraph ——→ **A. First main idea**

    1. First supporting detail

    2. Second supporting detail

    3. Third supporting detail

support, explain, and give more information about main idea of essay

B. Second main idea

    1. First supporting detail

    2. Second supporting detail

    3. Third supporting detail

same as paragraph A

C. Third main idea

    1. First supporting detail

    2. Second supporting detail

    3. Third supporting detail

same as paragraphs A and B

III. Conclusion

restates main ideas of body paragraphs ——→ **A. Brief summary of main ideas**

begins to wrap up essay ——→ **B. Other related statement**

ends the essay ——→ **C. Closing statement**

wrap up essay

Drafting
Write

Writing Paragraphs

A paragraph is a group of related sentences. The main idea of a paragraph is usually in the first sentence, called the **topic sentence**. The rest of the sentences in a paragraph give more information about the topic sentence. Start with the idea you want your audience to know. This will become the topic sentence for your paragraph. For example, let's say your essay is an expository piece about horses. You have gathered information about horses and made a web to put your information in order.

Your web may look something like this:

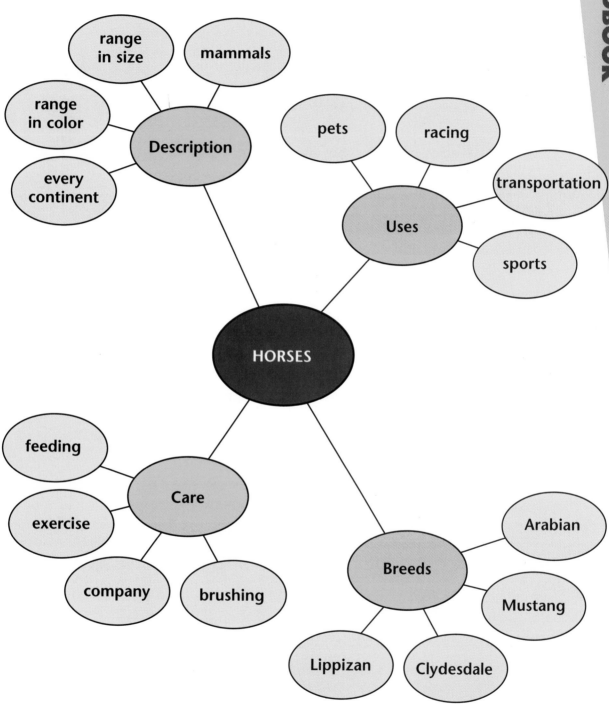

range in size

mammals

range in color

every continent

Description

pets

racing

transportation

Uses

sports

HORSES

feeding

exercise

company

brushing

Care

Breeds

Arabian

Mustang

Lippizan

Clydesdale

Take one part of your web—Breeds. Write it as a sentence. You might come up with this:

There are many different kinds, or breeds, of horses.

This is now your topic sentence. Now it's time to tell your audience more information about the main idea. If you have gathered information about horses, you might have these facts.

1. Arabian horses were prized by Bedouin tribes in the desert for their speed, beauty, and intelligence.
2. The Mustang is a well-known breed in North America and descends from Spanish horses.
3. The Clydesdale is native to Scotland and is one of the largest breeds.
4. The Lippizan horses were bred for the royal family of Spain, who valued them for their dazzling white coats, graceful appearance, and gentleness.

When you combine your topic sentence with these supporting sentences, you have a paragraph.

There are many different kinds, or breeds, of horses. Arabian horses were prized by Bedouin tribes in the desert for their speed, beauty, and intelligence. The Mustang is a well-known breed in North America and descends from Spanish horses. The Clydesdale is native to Scotland and is one of the largest breeds. The Lippizan horses were bred for the royal family of Spain, who valued them for their dazzling white coats, graceful appearance, and gentleness.

Following the same steps for the other three parts of your web will give you three more paragraphs. Put these together, and you will have the body of a well-organized essay. All you need now is an introduction and a conclusion. For tips about writing good introductions and conclusions see "Writing a Five-Paragraph Essay" on page HB20.

Writing a Five-Paragraph Essay

An essay is a piece of nonfiction writing about one topic. In grades 5 and 6, you practice writing a descriptive essay, a compare-and-contrast essay, a cause-and-effect essay, and a persuasive essay. Essays are made up of three basic parts—the introduction, the body, and the conclusion.

Write the body of your essay first. It doesn't matter that you don't have an introduction yet. It's very difficult to write a good introduction until you have written the body. Imagine trying to introduce a person you don't know to an audience. What would you say? That's kind of what it's like to try writing an introduction first. You don't know your essay yet. Write the body first and then you'll know what to say in your introduction.

Body

The body of your essay is where you explain, describe, prove, and give information about your main idea. Look at your graphic organizer. There's a good chance that you already have the makings of several good paragraphs.

Let's pretend you're writing a descriptive essay on your favorite vacation spot—the beach. After gathering and organizing your information, you may have three main points in your graphic organizer—how it looks, how it feels, and how it sounds. Look at the web on page HB21.

To move from one paragraph to the next, use a trick good writers know. It's called a "signal word." There's a list of these words on page HB41.

Once you have written all the paragraphs of the body of your essay, it's time to write the introduction and the conclusion.

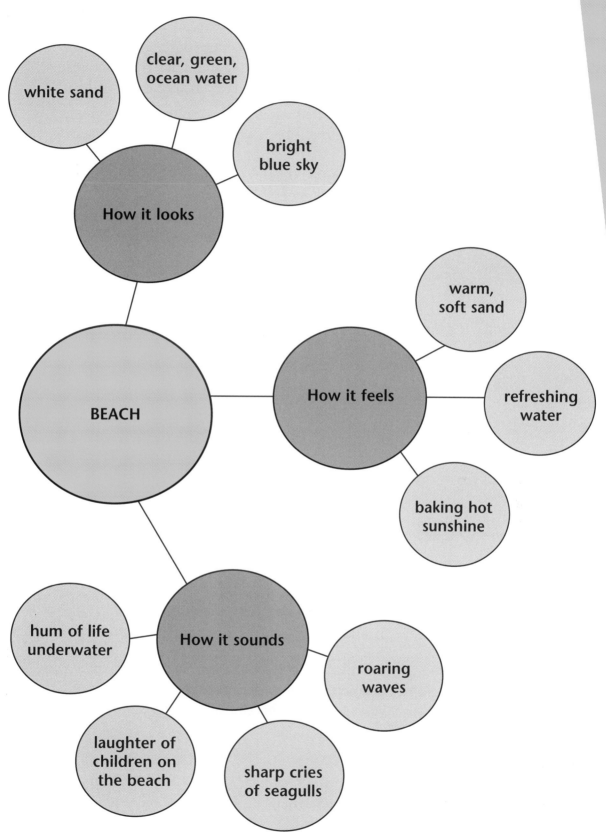

Introduction

The introduction is the first part of the essay that your audience will read or hear. You want it to get their attention and make them interested enough to keep reading or listening. You don't want to give away what's in the essay.

The Upside-Down Pyramid

If your introduction were a graphic organizer, it would look like an upside-down pyramid with more general information at the beginning and more specific information at the end. Let's write an introduction for our descriptive essay about the beach.

The first sentence of your introduction should say something true but general about your topic.

There are many great places to go on vacation.

This sentence gives some examples of vacation spots. It's still pretty general, but it gets closer to the main idea.

Amusement parks, campgrounds, and cities are some good choices for vacation spots.

This sentence should be the main idea of your essay.

For the sights, the sounds, and feeling good, nothing beats my favorite vacation spot—the beach.

Here's the complete introduction:

There are many great places to go on vacation. Amusement parks, campgrounds, and cities are some good choices for vacation spots. For the sights, the sounds, and feeling good, nothing beats my favorite vacation spot—the beach.

Remember—start with something general and true. Then say something a little more specific. Finish with the main idea of the essay. Now your introduction is complete.

Conclusion

The conclusion of an essay does two things. It restates the main idea of the essay, and it wraps up the essay. Restating the main idea is important. You want to make sure your audience remembers what the essay was about. Wrapping things up helps the audience feel that they have read a complete work and that nothing is missing.

The Right-Side-Up Pyramid

If the introduction of your essay looks like an upside-down pyramid, the conclusion looks like a pyramid right-side-up with more specific information at the beginning and more general information at the end. Here's how:

The first sentence of the conclusion should restate the main idea.

The beach is an amazing place to go on vacation if you want to see beautiful things, hear interesting and fun sounds, and feel great.

The next sentence should say something a little more general but still stay on the main idea.

It's a good idea to visit different and interesting places on vacation.

The final sentence should wrap things up and finish the essay. It should be very general.

Beaches all over the world offer a wonderful way to relax and enjoy your vacation.

When you put your conclusion together, it will look like this:

The beach is an amazing place to go on vacation if you want to see beautiful things, hear interesting and fun sounds, and feel great. It's a good idea to visit different and interesting places on vacation. Beaches all over the world offer a wonderful way to relax and enjoy your vacation.

Writing Poetry

Poetry is different from other forms of writing. Some poems are written in lines and stanzas and follow a rhyme or rhythm. Some poems are simply words or phrases with no rhyme. Most poems are full of imagery or word pictures. Whatever form a poem takes, it's one of the most creative forms of writing.

When you start to write a poem, the first thing to do is to pick a subject. It's a good idea to pick a subject that you know something about or a subject that means a lot to you. Next you should try to write down interesting ideas about your subject. You can write down your ideas however you like.

Then it is time to write your first draft. Once again, you can use any form you like to write your poem. Be sure to use plenty of descriptive words, or words that describe sounds, smells, tastes, and how things look and feel. As you begin to write, your poem might already be taking on its own form.

Revising is an important part of all writing, including writing poetry. You'll probably revise your poem many times. You might want to try changing the form of your poem. Once it's written, you may think it would be better stated in rhyme. You may think your poem is better if it doesn't rhyme. Just make sure your poem's message and ideas are clear to your readers.

Once you have written your final version, read it over to yourself. Then read it out loud. You may find more areas to improve.

Types of Poetry

Ballad: A ballad tells a story. Ballads are usually written as quatrains (four-line stanzas). Often, the first and third lines have four accented syllables; the second and fourth have three.

Blank Verse: Blank verse poems do not rhyme, but they have meter. Beginning with the second syllable of a line, every other syllable is accented.

Epic: An epic is a long poem that tells a story. The story describes adventures of heroes.

Free Verse: Free verse poems do not rhyme and do not have meter.

Haiku: Haiku is a form of poetry developed in Japan. The words of a haiku poem represent nature. A haiku is three lines in length. The first line is five syllables; the second is seven syllables; and the third is five syllables in length.

Limerick: A limerick is a funny poem that has five lines. Lines one, two, and five rhyme and have three stressed syllables. Lines three and four rhyme and have two stressed syllables.

Lyric: A lyric is a short poem that expresses personal feeling.

Ode: An ode is a long lyric. It expresses deeper feelings and uses poetic devices and imagery.

Sonnet: A sonnet is a fourteen-line poem that expresses personal feeling. Each line in a sonnet is ten syllables in length; every other syllable is stressed, beginning with the second syllable.

Poetry Terms

Alliteration: Alliteration is the repeating of the beginning consonant sounds:

> **c**ute, **c**uddly, **c**alico **c**ats

End Rhyme: End rhyme refers to the rhyming words at the ends of two or more lines of poetry:

> Her favorite pastime was to take a **hike**.
> His first choice was to ride a **bike**.

Foot: A foot is one unit of meter.

Meter: Meter is the pattern of accented and unaccented syllables in the lines of a traditional poem.

Onomatopoeia: Onomatopoeia is the use of a word whose sound makes you think of its meaning. Here are some examples:

> bang, beep, buzz, clang, swish, thump, zoom

Quatrain: A quatrain is a four-line stanza:

> At night she looks up at the stars
> And thinks of what might be.
> By day she works and studies so
> To someday live her dreams.

Stanza: A stanza is a section in a poem named for the number of lines it contains.

Verse: Verse is a name for a line of traditional poetry.

Revising
Elaborate and Clarify

Thesaurus

When it comes to saying things in different, more interesting ways, the thesaurus is one of the best friends a writer can have.

A thesaurus is a reference book that lists the *synonyms* (words that have the same or similar meaning) of words, and the *antonyms* (words that have the opposite meaning) of words.

Many times writers get stuck using the same words over and over. It's difficult to think of new and more colorful words. The next time you are writing, ask yourself, "Have I used a word too many times? Is there a better way to say this?" Chances are, the answer will be yes. That's where a thesaurus can help.

For example, let's say you are writing a descriptive essay about a place, and you have picked a beach where you vacationed last summer. You have written that the ocean was **beautiful**. You have said that the sky was a **beautiful** shade of blue. You have stated that the tropical plants were **beautiful**. Do you see a pattern yet?

All those things were beautiful, but there are more colorful words you can use. Maybe the ocean is **stunning** or **spectacular**. The sky might be a **lovely** or even an **exquisite** shade of blue. And how about those tropical plants? Are they **extravagant, magnificent,** or **dramatic** in their beauty? Use rich words and your writing becomes truly **fabulous**.

Dictionary

One of the most helpful tools for writers is the dictionary. Just think of it! Every word you could possibly need is in there. Until now, you might have used your dictionary only to look up the spellings of difficult words. That's important because good spelling makes writing clearer, but it's not the only information in a dictionary.

Your dictionary contains valuable information, such as the history of words, a guide for pronunciation, foreign words and phrases, the names of historical people, the names of places in the world, and lots of other interesting things. Some dictionaries even contain the Declaration of Independence and the Constitution of the United States! The next time you are looking for more than just the spelling of a word, try your dictionary.

Web Sites

With the help of an adult, try these Web sites for even more help in building your vocabulary and making your writing richer and clearer.

http://www.writetools.com
This is a one-stop Web site for writers. It contains links to reference materials, almanacs, calendars, historical documents, government resources, grammar and style guides, and all kinds of other tools for writing and editing.

http://www.bartleby.com
This Web site has links to several on-line dictionaries, encyclopedias, thesauri, and many other useful and interesting sources. It also contains links to on-line fiction and nonfiction books. It's like having a library of your own.

Capitalization

Capitalize:

- the first word in a sentence.
- all proper nouns, including people's names and the names of particular places.
- titles of respect.
- family titles used just before people's names and titles of respect that are part of names.
- initials of names.
- place names.
- proper adjectives, adjectives that are made from proper nouns.
- the months of the year and the days of the week.
- important words in the names of organizations.
- important words in the names of holidays.
- the first word in the greeting or closing of a letter.
- the word *I*.
- the first, last, and most important words in a title. Be sure to capitalize all verbs including *is* and *was*.
- the first word in a direct quotation.

Sentence Structure

The Sentence

A sentence is a group of words that tells a complete thought. A sentence has two parts: a **subject** and a **predicate**.

- The complete subject tells who or what.
  A famous artist painted the picture.

- The complete predicate tells what happened.
  A famous artist **painted the picture**.

Subject

The **subject** of a sentence tells whom or what the sentence is about.

- The **complete** subject includes all the words that name and tell about the subject.

  A **famous artist** painted the picture.

- The **simple** subject is the most important noun or pronoun in the complete subject.

  A famous **artist** painted the picture.

- A sentence can have one subject.

  Jessica walked home.

- A sentence can have a **compound** subject, two or more subjects that share the same predicate.

  Jessica and Joan walked home.

Predicate

The **predicate** of a sentence tells what happened.
The **complete** predicate includes a verb and all the words that tell what happened.

- A **complete** predicate can tell what the subject of the sentence did. This kind of predicate includes an action verb.

  A famous artist **painted the picture**.

- A complete predicate can also tell more about the subject. This kind of predicate includes a **linking verb**.

  The coat **was** red wool.

- A **predicate noun** follows a linking verb and renames the subject.

  The garment was **a coat**.

- A **predicate adjective** follows a linking verb and describes the subject.

  The coat was **red**.

- A **compound** predicate is two or more predicates that share the same subject. Compound predicates are often joined by the conjunction *and* or *or*.

    James **ran** across the deck and **jumped** into the pool.

- The **simple** predicate is the most important word or words in the complete predicate. The simple predicate is always a verb.

    A famous artist **painted** the picture.

Simple, Compound, and Complex Sentences

- A **simple** sentence tells one complete thought.

    A famous artist painted the picture.

- A **compound** sentence is made up of two simple sentences joined by a comma and a conjunction *(and, or, but)*. The two simple sentences in a compound sentence can also be joined by a semicolon. Two simple sentences can go together to make one compound sentence if the ideas in the simple sentences are related.

    Tony cut out the letters, **and** Shanna glued them to the poster.

- A **complex** sentence is made up of one **independent clause** (or simple sentence), and at least one **dependent clause**. A **dependent clause** is a group of words that has a subject and a predicate but cannot stand on its own.

    Dependent Clause: while Shanna glued them to the poster
    Independent Clause: Tony cut out the letters
    Complex Sentence: Tony cut out the letters, while Shanna glued them to the poster.

Subject-Verb Agreement

- The subject and its verb must agree in number.
  One **part** of speech **is** a noun.
  (*Part* is singular; it requires the verb *is*.)

  The **sweatshirts** on the rack **were** on sale.
  (*Sweatshirts* is plural; it requires the verb *were*.)

- Sometimes a **helping verb** is needed to help the main verb show action. A helping verb comes before a main verb.
  Joe **has watched** the team practice.

- An **action verb** shows action in a sentence.
  A penguin **waddles** and **slides** on the ice.

- A **linking verb** does not show action. It connects the subject of a sentence to a word or words in the predicate that tell about the subject. Linking verbs include *am, is, are, was,* and *were. Seem* and *become* are linking verbs, too.
  The coat **is** red wool.
  This milk **seems** sour.

Abbreviations

Abbreviations are shortened forms of words. Many abbreviations begin with a capital letter and end with a period.

Abbreviate:

- titles of address and titles of respect.
    Mister (Mr. Robert Sing)
    Mistress (Mrs. Amy Walters)
    Doctor (Dr. Donna Rodrigues)

- words used in addresses.
    Street (St.)
    Avenue (Ave.)
    Route (Rt.)
    Boulevard (Blvd.)
    Road (Rd.)

- certain words in the names of businesses.
    Incorporated (Inc.)
    Corporation (Corp.)
    Limited (Ltd.)

- days of the week when you take notes.
    Sunday (Sun.)
    Monday (Mon.)
    Tuesday (Tues.)
    Wednesday (Wed.)
    Thursday (Thurs.)
    Friday (Fri.)
    Saturday (Sat.)

- most months of the year.
    January (Jan.)
    February (Feb.)
    March (Mar.)
    April (Apr.)
    August (Aug.)
    September (Sept.)
    October (Oct.)
    November (Nov.)
    December (Dec.)
  (May, June, and July do not have abbreviated forms.)

- directions.
    North (N)
    East (E)
    South (S)
    West (W)

Quotation Marks

Quotation marks are used to separate a speaker's exact words from the rest of the sentence. Begin a **direct quotation** with a capital letter. Use a comma to separate the direct quotation from the speaker's name. When a direct quotation comes at the end of a sentence, put the end mark inside the last quotation mark. When writing a conversation, begin a new paragraph with each change of speaker. For example:

Tim said, "My homework is done." He was hoping to go rollerblading before dinner.

"You can go," his mom answered. "Just be back before dinnertime."

End Marks

Every sentence must end with a **period,** an **exclamation point,** or a **question mark**.

- Use a **period** at the end of a statement (declarative sentence) or a command (imperative sentence).
    Statement: The sky is blue.
    Command: Please come here.

- Use an **exclamation point** at the end of a firm command (imperative sentence)
    Shut the door!

    or at the end of a sentence that shows great feeling or excitement (exclamatory sentence)
    It's hot!

- Use a **question mark** at the end of an asking sentence (interrogative sentence).
    Is it raining?

Commas

Use a **comma:**

- after an introductory word in a sentence.
  Wow, you're here.

- to separate items in a series. Put the last comma before *and* or *or*.
  Jessica bought paper, pens, and a pencil.

- when speaking directly to a person.
  Alan, take your seat.

- to separate a direct quotation from the speaker's name.
  Tim said, "My homework is done."

- with the conjunctions *and, or,* or *but* when combining independent clauses in a compound sentence.
  He could play soccer, or he could run track.

Parts of Speech

Nouns

- A **singular noun** names one person, place, thing, or idea.
  boy   watch   cat

- A **plural noun** names more than one person, place, thing or idea.
  To make most singular nouns plural, add *-s.*
  boys   cats

- For nouns ending in *sh, ch, x,* or *z,* add *-es* to make the word plural.
  watch/watches   box/boxes

- For nouns ending in a consonant and *y,* change the *y* to *i* and add *-es.*
  pony/ponies   story/stories

- For many nouns that end in *f* or *fe,* replace *f* or *fe* with *ves* to make the noun plural.
  hoof/hooves   shelf/shelves

- Some words change spelling when the plural is formed.
  man/men   child/children

- Some words have the same singular and plural form.
  deer/deer   fish/fish

Possessive Nouns

A **possessive noun** shows ownership.

- To make a singular noun possessive, add an apostrophe and -*s*.

  boy/boy's   cat/cat's   watch/watch's

- When a singular noun ends in *s*, add an apostrophe and -*s*.

  dress/dress's   class/class's

- To make a plural noun that ends in *s* possessive, add an apostrophe.

  boys/boys'   cats/cats'   watches/watches'

- When a plural noun does not end in *s*, add an apostrophe and -*s* to show possession.

  women/women's   children/children's

Verbs

Verbs can tell about the present, the past, or the future.

- The **present tense** is used to show that something happens regularly or is true now.

  Add -*s* to most verbs to show present tense when the subject is *he, she, it,* or a singular noun.

  He walks to school.

  Add -*es* to verbs ending in *s, ch, sh, x,* or *z*.

  Joe watches the team practice.

  Do not add -*s* or -*es* if the subject is a plural noun or *I, you, we,* or *they*.

  I want to go to the park.

  Change *y* to *i* and add -*es* to form some present tense verbs.

  Sam hurries to school.

- The **past tense** shows past action. Add *-ed* to most verbs to form the past tense.

  climb/climbed   watch/watched   show/showed

- Past tense verbs that do not add *-ed* are called **irregular verbs**.

Present	Past	Past Participle (with *have, has,* or *had*)
bring	brought	brought
go	went	gone
grow	grew	grown
know	knew	known
take	took	taken

- The **future tense** indicates future action. Use the helping verb *will* to form the future tense.

  Joe will watch the team practice.

- The **present perfect tense** shows action that began in the past and may still be happening. To form the present perfect tense, add the helping verb *has* or *have* to the past participle of a verb.

  Joe has watched the team practice.

Pronouns

A **pronoun** can replace a **noun** naming a person, place, thing, or idea. Personal pronouns include *I, me, you, we, us, he, she, it, they,* and *them.*

- A **subject** pronoun takes the place of the subject of a sentence. Subject pronouns are said to be in the **subjective case**. Do not use both the pronoun and the noun it replaces together.

  Incorrect: Marla she answered the question.
  Correct: Marla answered the question.

- An **object** pronoun replaces a noun that is the object of a verb or preposition. Object pronouns are said to be in the **objective case**.

    Rosco came with **us**.

- Use a **subject** pronoun as part of a **compound subject**. Use an **object** pronoun as part of a **compound object**. To test whether a pronoun is correct, say the sentence *without* the other part of a compound subject or object.

    Incorrect: Rosco and **him** came with Jessica and **we**.
    Correct: Rosco and **he** came with Jessica and **us**.

- An **antecedent** is the word or phrase a pronoun refers to. The antecedent always includes a noun.

    Joan cleaned **her** room.

- A pronoun must match its antecedent. An antecedent and pronoun agree when they have the same **number** (singular or plural) and **gender** (male or female).

- **Possessive** pronouns show ownership. The words *my, your, his, her, its, their,* and *our* are possessive pronouns.

- The **interrogative** pronouns *who, what,* and *which* are used to ask questions.

    Who opened the window?

- *This, that, these,* and *those* can be used as **demonstrative** pronouns. Use *this* and *these* to talk about one or more things that are nearby. Use *that* and *those* to talk about one or more things that are far away.

    This is interesting.
    That is his new car.
    Those are my favorite.

Prepositions

A **preposition** shows a relationship between a word in a sentence and a noun or pronoun that follows the preposition. Prepositions help tell *when, where, what kind, how,* or *how much.*

Common Prepositions

aboard	behind	from	throughout
about	below	in	to
above	beneath	into	toward
across	beside	like	under
after	between	near	underneath
against	beyond	of	until
along	but (except)	off	unto
amid	by	on	up
among	down	over	upon
around	during	past	with
at	except	since	within
before	for	through	without

Conjunctions

The words *and, or,* and *but* are **coordinating conjunctions**.

- Coordinating conjunctions may be used to join words within a sentence.

    Jessica bought paper, pens, **and** a pencil.

- A comma and a coordinating conjunction can be used to join two or more simple sentences.

    Tony cut out the letters**, and** Shanna glued them to the poster.

Negatives

A negative word says "no" or "not."

- Often negatives are in the form of contractions.
  isn't, doesn't, haven't

- It is not correct to use two negatives to refer to the same thing.
  Incorrect: Tina **hasn't never** seen the ocean.
  Correct: Tina **hasn't ever** seen the ocean.

Homophones

Homophones are words that sound alike but have different spellings and meanings.

- Here is a list of some homophones often confused in writing.

are	**Are** is a form of the verb *be*.
our	**Our** is a possessive noun.
hour	An **hour** is sixty minutes.
its	**Its** is a possessive pronoun.
it's	**It's** is a contraction of the words *it is*.
there	**There** means "in that place." It can also be used as an introductory word.
their	**Their** is a possessive pronoun. It shows something belongs to more than one person or thing.
they're	**They're** is a contraction made from the words *they are*.
two	**Two** is a number.
to	**To** means "toward."
too	**Too** means "also." **Too** can mean "more than enough."
your	**Your** is a possessive pronoun.
you're	**You're** is a contraction made from the words *you are*.
whose	**Whose** is a possessive pronoun.
who's	**Who's** is a contraction made from the words *who* and *is* or *who* and *has*.

ate	**Ate** is a form of the verb *eat*.
eight	**Eight** is a number word.
principal	A **principal** is a person with authority.
principle	A **principle** is a general rule or code of behavior.
waist	The **waist** is the middle part of the body.
waste	To **waste** something is to use it in a careless way.
aloud	**Aloud** means out loud, or able to be heard.
allowed	**Allowed** is a form of the verb *allow*.

Signal Words

Signal words help writers move from one idea to another. Here is a list of some common signal words.

Time-Order Signal Words

after	third	later	as soon as
before	till	immediately	when
during	until	finally	then
first	meanwhile	soon	next
second			

Comparison/Contrast Signal Words

in the same way	likewise	as	also
similarly	like	as well	
but	however	otherwise	yet
still	even though	although	on the other hand

Concluding or Summarizing Signal Words

as a result	finally	in conclusion	to sum up
therefore	lastly	in summary	all in all

Writing a Letter

Friendly Letters

A friendly letter is an informal letter written to a friend or family member. In a friendly letter, you might send a message, invite someone to a party, or thank someone for a gift. A friendly letter has five parts:

- The **heading** gives your address and the date.
- The **greeting** includes the name of the person you are writing to. It begins with a capital letter and ends with a comma.
- The **body** of the letter gives your message.
- The **closing** is a friendly or polite way to say good-bye. It begins with a capital letter and ends with a comma.
- The **signature** is your name.

Business Letters

A business letter is a formal letter. You would write a business letter to a company, an employer, a newspaper, or any person you do not know well. A business letter looks a lot like a friendly letter, but a business letter includes the name and address of the business you are writing to. The greeting of a business letter begins with a capital letter and ends with a **colon (:)**.

Addressing Letters

The envelope below shows how to address a letter. A friendly letter and a business letter are addressed the same way.

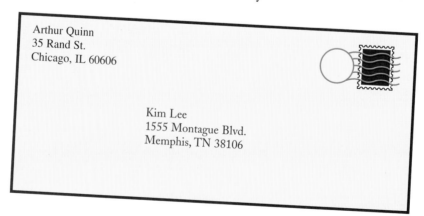

Arthur Quinn
35 Rand St.
Chicago, IL 60606

Kim Lee
1555 Montague Blvd.
Memphis, TN 38106

Publishing
Share

This is the last step of the writing process. You have gathered and organized information. You have drafted, revised, and edited your writing. Your project is completed. Here are some tips for publishing your work.

Ways to Publish

There are lots of ways to publish your work. Keep your audience in mind as you choose different publishing methods. Your teacher might ask you to publish your work by writing your final draft on a clean piece of paper, with a title and your name at the top. You might try one of the publishing methods from this book, like an author's circle or a letter with an addressed envelope. It all depends on who is going to read or listen to your work.

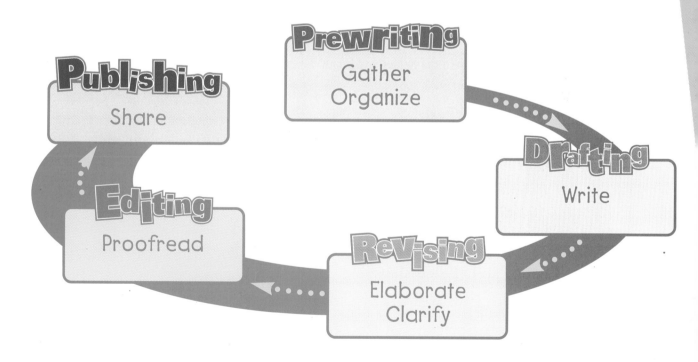

Publishing
Share

Prewriting
Gather
Organize

Drafting
Write

Revising
Elaborate
Clarify

Editing
Proofread

Listening, Speaking, and Thinking Skills

Listening

These tips will help you be a good listener:

- Listen carefully when others are speaking.

- Keep in mind your reason for listening. Are you listening to learn about a topic? To be entertained? To get directions? Decide what you should get out of the listening experience.

- Look directly at the speaker. Doing this will help you concentrate on what he or she has to say.

- Do not interrupt the speaker or talk to others while the speaker is talking.

- Ask questions when the speaker is finished talking if there is anything you did not understand.

Speaking

Being a good speaker takes practice. These guidelines can help you become an effective speaker.

Giving Oral Reports

- Be prepared. Know exactly what you are going to talk about and how long you will speak. Have your notes in front of you.

- Speak slowly and clearly. Speak loudly enough so everyone can hear you.

- Look at your audience.

Taking Part in Discussions

- Listen to what others have to say.

- Disagree politely. Let others in the group know you respect their points of view.

- Try not to interrupt others. Everyone should have a chance to speak.

Thinking

Writers use a variety of thinking skills as they work through the writing process. These skills include **logic, analyzing, setting goals, creativity, and problem solving**. As you write, keep these skills in mind and try to put them to use as much as possible.

- **Logic** Writers use logic to support a point of view by using reasoning, facts, and examples.

- **Analyzing** Analyzing is a thinking skill that requires the writer to think about and examine the information learned about a topic. Once the information is examined, a general conclusion or more meaningful understanding can be made about the topic.

- **Setting Goals** When setting goals, writers must think about deadlines (when the assignment is due; how much time there is for prewriting, drafting, revising, editing, and publishing), the objective of the writing assignment, and the amount of research required.

- **Creativity** Using creativity means using the imagination. Writers let their minds wonder about many different ways to tackle an assignment before finally settling on one. It is often necessary to start an assignment, stop, try it a different way, stop again, and maybe even go back to the original idea. Thinking creatively and openly allows the writer to examine many options.

- **Problem Solving** Learning to problem solve helps writers make decisions about the writing assignment and helps them use facts and opinions correctly. Strategies for problem solving include: naming the problem; thinking of everything about the problem; thinking of ways to solve the problem; choosing the best plan to solve the problem and trying it out; and analyzing the result.